Leadership
TEAMING

The Superintendent-Principal Relationship

Cathie E. West
Mary Lynne Derrington

CORWIN PRESS
A SAGE Company

For information:

Corwin Press
A SAGE Company
2455 Teller Road
Thousand Oaks, California 91320
www.corwinpress.com

SAGE India Pvt. Ltd.
B 1/I 1 Mohan Cooperative
  Industrial Area
Mathura Road, New Delhi
India 110 044

SAGE Ltd.
1 Oliver's Yard
55 City Road
London EC1Y 1SP
United Kingdom

SAGE Asia-Pacific Pte. Ltd.
33 Pekin Street #02-01
Far East Square
Singapore 048763

Printed in the United States of America

Library of Congress Cataloging-in-Publication Data

West, Cathie E.
Leadership teaming : the superintendent-principal relationship / Cathie E. West,
Mary Lynne Derrington.
        p. cm.
Includes bibliographical references and index.
ISBN 978-1-4129-6630-6 (cloth)
ISBN 978-1-4129-6631-3 (pbk.)
    1. Principal-superintendent relationships. 2. School superintendents—Professional relationships. 3. School principals—Professional relationships. 4. School management teams. I. Derrington, Mary Lynne. II. Title.

LB2831.7.W47 2009
371.2′011—dc22   2008022901

This book is printed on acid-free paper.

08   09   10   11   12   10   9   8   7   6   5   4   3   2   1

Acquisitions Editor:	Hudson Perigo
Editorial Assistant:	Lesley K. Blake
Production Editor:	Amy Schroller
Copy Editor:	Alison Hope
Typesetter:	C&M Digitals (P) Ltd.
Proofreader:	Dorothy Hoffman
Indexer:	Judy Hunt
Cover Designer:	Rose Storey

Leadership
TEAMING

*To the superb superintendent-principal teams across this country
who make "teamwork" a rewarding reality.*

Contents

Preface

SUPERINTENDENT'S PERSPECTIVE

Mary Lynne Derrington

We hadn't seen each other for many years when we met that August. After hugs, smiles and catching up, we discovered that both of us had been in several other school districts since we last worked together. In fact, between Cathie West's thirty years of experience as a principal and my eighteen years at the superintendent level, our combined administrative experience covered thirteen school districts. Reflecting on what made some experiences memorable and rewarding and others mediocre or challenging, we reached the same conclusion: the most rewarding and successful school districts had the most effective leadership teams. Specifically, it was the leadership team consisting of the principal and the superintendent and the relationship between these two administrators that created either a healthy or harmful working environment. We acknowledged that neither of us had any training in our preparation or inservice programs on how to develop this important relationship. We agreed that we could contribute to the field and assist others in learning from our experiences.

We live life forward but understand our experiences backward. We spent the next two years reflecting and searching for answers and information to describe the critical attributes of the superintendent-principal relationship.

Why I Wrote This Book

Reflecting on my experiences, I believe that becoming a superintendent was akin to becoming a new driver. I learned the rules of the road, passed the test, and had some hours in guided practice behind the wheel. However, once I was alone behind the wheel and steering without feedback, I lacked the refined judgment that experience develops. I was prone to driving fast and missing important signals.

Likewise, as a new superintendent I cognitively knew the job and felt prepared for the challenge. But as an inexperienced "driver," I sometimes ignored warning signals and proceeded too quickly for conditions. Most important, I knew little about developing the critical relationships that support a successful superintendent-principal team. I have found from talking with many other superintendents that this novice experience is not unusual. Like the new driver, you find yourself in control overnight. One changes from being a principal to becoming the supervisor of administrators who yesterday were peers. The expectations others have of you can change in just twenty-four hours.

Fortunately, I learned quickly. I learned that leadership is a team sport. I learned that the complex job of a superintendent can be done only with the goodwill and good thinking of the principals. I learned that the demands of leadership necessitate creating and building the superintendent-principal team. And I learned that building this team requires a set of skills not typically taught but universally expected.

This book is a vehicle through which to share insights and lessons learned, sometimes the hard way, frequently in a moment of enlightenment. This book is also the result of a gift of time. After twenty-five years in administration, I was blessed with a university position that provides the opportunity to research effective teams and reflect on effective practices.

What You Will Learn

There are tremendous demands placed on superintendents by all stakeholders, including principals. I see the frustrations of principals when the superintendent relationship fails to bring about team cohesiveness. I hope to give both principals and superintendents concepts to ponder and suggestions for unleashing the power of the superintendent-principal team. From my perspective, this is the most important team in a school district. It is this team that ultimately determines the schooling outcomes of young people in communities across this country.

PRINCIPAL'S PERSPECTIVE

Cathie E. West

I was a young student back in the 1950s and my memories of that difficult time run deep—as if I had known back then that hanging tight to what I had heard, seen, and felt would make a difference later. My classrooms were sterile, the curriculum lifeless, and the teachers cold and unapproachable. Their no-nonsense approach to teaching and discipline was so deadening that, despite my immaturity, I knew something was very wrong in my school house. Decades later I became a principal so that I could run my own school. I pictured cheerful classrooms, loving teachers, and a spirited curriculum. Students would thrive, as would their teachers, and—if I did my job right—my unsettling past would open the door to better schooling for today's children.

I have been a principal now for thirty years, have experienced the evolution of the principalship from manager to instructional leader, and responded to ever-changing demands. My work has been unrelentingly challenging, remarkably stimulating, and extraordinarily rewarding.

However, being a principal has been tougher than I expected. I have found more work to do than I could ever hope to accomplish, teachers who are incompetent, students who are dangerous, and parents who are just plain crazy. I've lived with crisis du jour, tangled with malevolent unions, endured mean-spirited school board members, and suffered from the decisions of clueless bureaucrats at all levels. Sadly, along the way there has been little in the way of help. Nevertheless, after all these years, I love being a principal and feel honored and proud to do this job.

Why I Wrote This Book

As I traveled the pathway to principal success, I discovered the most telling marker in regard to my effectiveness—my boss, the school district superintendent. I have worked for a dozen superintendents and know firsthand how their outlook on life, competency level, and capacity to lead affects the perceptions, performance, and confidence of their principals. Whatever the quality of the superintendent, I also discovered that doing my best work required getting the most out of our relationship. This meant building a strong alliance, working collaboratively, and supporting each other's work. In other words, it meant becoming a superlative team.

What You Will Learn

For my part in the book, I covered concepts and strategies that will help superintendents work more effectively with their principals, the people whose work underlies their own success. For principals, I included both good and bad stories from the trenches. The "bad stories" about superintendent-principal relationship gone awry are meant to be instructive. The "good stories" about relationships that thrived will show principals how to forge powerful alliances with their superintendents.

ABOUT OUR BOOK

We look at the leadership team from two perspectives—that of the principal and that of the superintendent. The reader will hear two voices addressing four major themes: leadership teaming, leadership qualities, leadership team essentials, and leadership learning. Chapters alternate between these voices, with the superintendent speaking about the theme first after which the principal adds her voice on the same theme. Like the six blind men describing the elephant, we sometimes grabbed on to a different part. In the final analysis, however, we describe the entire animal. Each of us identifies critical team components from her unique set of experiences, research read, and studies undertaken. We also describe team components from the perspective of our different leadership roles. Although each of our voices is unique, we share many views.

Special Features

At the conclusion of each chapter, Closing in on Key Concepts summarizes the big ideas. This is followed by Extending Your Thinking, which invites readers to apply what has been learned to their own team experience. Resource material is included so that administrators may implement suggested strategies.

Who This Book Is For

Taken as a whole, the book taps into the powerful forces at work in the superintendent-principal team and describes how to harness this energy to improve education for students. New superintendents and principals will find concepts and suggestions not typically taught in schools or seminars on how to form a superintendent-principal team. Experienced superintendents and principals will be able to reflect on their practice and project forward into new plans of action, and superintendent-principal teams will get the chance to discuss their responses to these critical questions:

What characterizes a superlative relationship between superintendent and principal?

What makes this team distinctly different from teams at all other levels in a school district?

Are there systems and strategies that support this effort?

How does the superintendent-principal team communicate, make decisions, and solve problems?

What insights can you share regarding the roles and management styles of both the superintendent and the principal in a team relationship?

This book is also for university instructors who wish to incorporate discussions about the leadership team into educational administration curriculum. We observe that this topic lacks attention in the preparation of both principals and superintendents.

Overview of the Contents

We bring the dual perspective of principal and superintendent to these pages. Each chapter provides a framework for understanding these viewpoints and their impact on team relationships. The reader will also find the means to equip oneself for success. The critical themes leadership teaming (Part I), leadership qualities (Part II), leadership team essentials (Part III), and leadership learning (Part IV) present vital team-building concepts, each of which is supported by vivid examples and practical tips. The reader will learn what effective teaming looks like and how to attain it.

Acknowledgments

This book is the result of the work and stories of many people. We would like to acknowledge some of the contributions that made this book possible. First, we express our deep appreciation to the many principals and superintendents who generously shared their precious time and colorful stories of success and failure. Some if these fine administrators are identified in this book, while others spoke to us anonymously from the sidelines. Each of these contributions served to bring this book to life, and for that we are grateful.

We are also indebted to Executive Editor Hudson Perigo who believed in our project from the start and who provided ongoing consultation and assistance. We extend this appreciation to Editorial Assistant Lesley Blake who patiently fielded our many e-mails and phone calls and who handled our manuscript with care. Finally, we thank our superb Copy Editor, Alison Hope, and our talented Production Editor, Amy Schroller, who shaped our manuscript into a book we can take pride in.

Corwin Press gratefully acknowledges the contributions of the following reviewers:

Irwin Blumer
Research Professor
Boston College
Chestnut Hill, MA

Liane Brouillette
Associate Professor
University of California, Irvine
Irvine, CA

Judy Brunner
Author and Trainer
Instructional Solutions Group
Springfield, MO

Teresa P. Cunningham
Principal, Laurel Elementary School
Johnson County School System
Mountain City, TN

Marcus J. Haack
Clinical Associate Professor, Educational
    Policy and Leadership Studies
University of Iowa
Iowa City, IA

Kari Henderson-Burke
Elementary Principal
Monte Cristo Elementary
Granite Falls, WA

Lynn Lisy-Macan
Superintendent
Cobleskill-Richmondville Central School District
Cobleskill, NY

Susan Printy
Associate Professor of Educational Administration
Michigan State University
East Lansing, MI

Joy Rose
High School Principal (Retired)
Westerville City Schools
Westerville, OH

About the Authors

 **Cathie E. West** has an MS degree in education and thirty years of experience as an elementary school principal. Currently she is the principal of Mountain Way Elementary School in Granite Falls, Washington. Cathie has been twice honored as an exemplary principal, receiving the Washington Distinguished Principal Award as the representative from Douglas County in 1998, and as the representative from Snohomish County in 2005. Cathie has taught at the college level, directed a wide variety of special programs, and coordinated curriculum and staff development for numerous school districts. In addition, she was an editorial advisor for the *National Association of Elementary School Principals* (2002–05) and now serves on the Editorial Board for *Washington State Kappan*. Cathie has written articles for *Principal, Communicator,* and *ERS Spectrum;* contributed to several books authored by Elaine McEwan; and served as manuscript reviewer for Corwin Press and Eye on Education. Cathie can be reached at CathieWest@verizon.net.

 **Mary Lynne Derrington, EdD,** has eighteen years of experience as a superintendent and seven as a principal. She is currently an assistant professor at Western Washington University in Bellingham, Washington. Mary Lynne is the author of publications in a wide variety of education journals including *Principal News, ERS Spectrum, The Executive Educator, The School Administrator, Curriculum in Context, School Information and Research Service,* and the *School Science and Mathematics Journal.* She is the editor of the *Washington State Kappan,* a journal for research, leadership and practice. Mary Lynne has cochaired Washington State education conferences for the Washington State Association of School Administrators and for Phi Delta Kappa, such as the recent Preparing Students for Citizenship in a Global World. She is past president of numerous professional organizations, including two Phi Delta Kappa chapters, Rotary International (East Jefferson, Washington), The American Heart Association (Clallam County, Washington), and the United Way Board (Jefferson County, Washington). Awards include a Fulbright Scholarship, Community Relations National Award from The School Planning and Management Organization, an Award of Merit from the

Washington Association of School Administrators, Meritorious Staff Development Program Award from the Washington State Staff Development Association, and a Rachel Royston Delta Kappa Gamma Scholarship for Outstanding Women in Education. Mary Lynne's current research includes the effective evaluation of principals using the Interstate School Leaders Licensure Consortium (ISLLC) standards and barriers and attractions to women who aspire to the superintendency. Mary Lynne can be contacted at MaryLynne .Derrington@wwu.edu.

PART I

Leadership Teaming

Part I of our book introduces the concept of leadership teaming and explores the significance of strong superintendent-principal relationships. Chapter 1 presents characteristics of quality teaming from the superintendent's perspective. Chapter 2 brings the principal's viewpoint to teaming by describing indicators of a supportive team culture and what superintendents do to lead principals effectively.

The Superintendent's Perspective

1

Characteristics of High-Quality Teams

Management is about people. All of management structure is directed toward one aim, allowing the individual to perform his or her job to the utmost while experiencing joy in his or her work in a manner consistent with the aims of the organization. It is a leader's job to foster joy in work, harmony and teamwork.

—Rafael Aguayo (1990, p. 181)

LEADERSHIP TEAMS WORK IN HARMONY

Benjamin Franklin observed that getting the thirteen separate colonies to act as one was like trying to get thirteen bells to chime at the same time. Similarly, the superintendent's leadership challenge is to take a diverse group of principals and create a team that works in accord. Harmony can quickly disintegrate into disharmony, especially when the voices of the district directors and other support staff are added to the symphony.

Although a district has many teams, the group that includes the superintendent and principals is arguably the most powerful. Their collective leadership impacts all students and staff in a district. These leaders intuitively understand the need for harmonious relationships to achieve goals that require working together. Less intuitive is knowledge of the specific steps required to create a harmonious district leadership team. How does a superintendent encourage team values among principals who view themselves first and foremost as their school's advocate?

Teams Work in Coordination

A superintendent told me a story about an elementary school that changed their ending day bell schedule by just three minutes, with unanticipated results. The school site council had developed a school improvement plan that reallocated time that students spent waiting in line for the bus to more time in the classroom. However, like a pebble dropped in a pool, those few minutes' difference created ripples throughout the district—throwing off the district bus schedule, decreasing teacher-negotiated planning time, making faculty late for afterschool intramurals supervision, and causing students to arrive home late to anxious parents. Within hours of the change, the unsuspecting superintendent was fielding phone calls from the union, receiving e-mails from upset parents, and being visited by the school board president, who had received complaints.

As this example illustrates, teams are organizational groups composed of members who are interdependent and who must coordinate their activities to accomplish their goals (Northouse, 2007). In interdependent work, as in the bell schedule example, actions taken by a team member principal could require a response by each of the other team members, including the superintendent.

The coordination of interdependent work is effectively accomplished through sound relationships, positive connections, and responsiveness to other team members. Forming and developing individual school leaders into a district team is the superintendent's responsibility. The superintendent takes a group of individually diverse and geographically separated school principals and forms a team through strategies that build knowledge of each other's work.

One strategy is to create shared knowledge of each principal's school operations and leadership activities. When team members share knowledge of each other's activities and how they fit together, the powerful bond of understanding develops. This understanding provides a context for considering any impact on the district that was brought on by a change or decision.

Recently I met with a group of regional superintendents. Together we generated examples of how an understanding of each other's schools could be developed. One superintendent of a large district creates a video of each school and shows it to the team as a way to illustrate current activities. Another organizes a shadow experience whereby principals from the secondary school spend a day in the elementary school and vice versa to "walk in each other's moccasins." Yet another forms teams of principals to "walk through" classrooms at schools around the district to observe curriculum in action and to talk with teachers.

Teams Model Collegiality

The leadership team is distinctly different from any other team in the school district. This team directly influences the entire school district's performance through policies and procedures. The leadership team influences all operations in a school district and makes decisions that affect the work and morale of all. The team impacts student learning in a hands-on daily operational fashion, not in the more removed policy-making role of the school board.

It follows, then, that the role of the superintendent in interactions with a team of leaders is distinctly different from that of any other team in the district. The superintendent becomes a facilitator of districtwide decisions alongside the principals and between the principals and the school board.

The role model impact is powerful, but I often observe a disconnect when the superintendent expects collegial behavior in the schools but does not create a similar atmosphere within the leadership team. Principals will recognize a superintendent's inconsistent behavior and report it to others. As a colleague once remarked to me, "You cannot mandate collaboration." The best way for a leader to mold collaboration in others is to model that behavior. Rivero (1998), an expert on executive team behavior, reported on the importance of a CEO's behavior as a model for developing subordinates. Team forming does not occur through control, but rather through a purposeful building of collegial relationships.

The superintendent-principal team functions in the spotlight of staff and community scrutiny. Thus, by the example demonstrated, the school staff has either an exemplary role model to emulate or a dysfunctional example to deride. The superintendent's behavior directly affects principals who may emulate the superintendent's actions with the school faculty.

VISION OF A LEADERSHIP TEAM

In junior high school, my English teacher noticed that I had difficulty reading words at a distance. He told my mother, who made an appointment with the optometrist. At this gawky, self-conscious, adolescent age, I was horrified at the thought of wearing glasses. I spent weeks in denial claiming that I could see a mosquito forty feet away. In the optometrist's office, I faked my way through the tests, or so I thought. Not fooled, however, the optometrist took me to the window and pointed in the direction of the park across the street.

"See them?" he asked.

I did see something moving, so answered affirmatively.

He reached up and put corrective lenses in front of my eyes and asked, "See them now?"

I recall crying at that moment, when I clearly saw children on swings. I had missed seeing them before and knew that meant I needed glasses. Along with dismay, I also felt relief. By fooling myself, I had missed much. My vision could be so much better and the tool to fix that was literally in front of my eyes.

The superintendent likewise needs a clear vision of what a well-functioning team looks like. We need to put the corrective lenses in front of our eyes to see both principals working as a team and the way this strengthens the outcomes across the district.

Looking Good on the Surface

Most superintendents believe they do have a collaborative and supportive team of principals. Unfortunately, their visions are not always reflected in reality (Nadler & Spencer, 1998). Much teamwork is "cosmetic": the trappings of teamwork are apparent, but the behavior of the team members reveals a lack of teamwork and negative relationships among individuals. Teams, like individuals, mask certain behaviors and beliefs in front of "the boss."

This became clear to me one day when I observed two different leadership teams in two different districts. As a participant in a state process on school improvement, I had been asked to provide information to groups in both districts. While waiting my turn during their meetings, I had ample time to unobtrusively watch team actions and interactions. I was struck by the apparent similarities of the teams in size, structure, agenda, and identified tasks, but was stunned by the differences in the covert behaviors and overt actions of the principals.

Principals in Team I surreptitiously doodled, had quiet side interactions with obviously allied principals, and showed little interest or curiosity in the topic presented. They showed a single-minded focus on their own schools, with no apparent concern for other schools or students, and they were resistant to each other's ideas. Some principals masked what they truly felt, and then later had conversations that indicated their frustration and lack of support for decisions that had been made.

Principals in Team II were engaged, exhibited relaxed and friendly body language, made comments relevant to the topic, provided positive support for other principals' comments, and demonstrated the ability and the desire to see each other's point of view. Both the superintendent and the principals interacted with many words and gestures of appreciation.

Cosmetic teamwork results when surface behaviors affirm the value of teamwork, but members interact in subgroups by complaining and acting noncollaboratively. Cosmetic collaboration occurs when a superintendent claims to want teamwork but is unwilling to give up any control. Thus, the appearance of a cohesive team is there in the presence of the superintendent, but nothing transfers to the day-to-day behaviors or beliefs of the individual team members. In addition to the relationship between the superintendent and each principal, superintendents build connections among principals by promoting high-quality relationships.

Developing Prosocial Teams

Increased research provides credibility for the importance of adult prosocial behavior at work, sometimes labeled "citizenship" in the literature (Cameron, Dutton, & Quinn, 2003). One important aspect of prosocial behavior is an emphasis on the positive. Positive teams value what each individual contributes to the group. In *Good to Great*, Collins (2001) emphasizes the need to get the right people on the bus. Many superintendents and principals interpret this as a license to get rid of negative or bothersome team members, and hire those more amenable to their own perspective. However, a closer reading of Collins does not support this view. Collins states that it would be a "tragic mistake" to think that wantonly swinging the ax is the way to greatness. Instead, superintendents take the team they have and capitalize on various strengths of the members.

Some principals will challenge your faith in this concept. Joe was an inspirational principal and motivator for his staff yet disengaged and unresponsive with his colleagues. Building on his strengths, we asked Joe to lead the development of a plan for team recognition and rewards. His behavior changed, perhaps only temporarily. Nevertheless, when he was positively engaged with his peers, morale lifted perceptibly.

Building a positive team relationship requires the superintendent to first believe that team relationships are important in reaching districtwide goals. Most superintendents advocate for a collaborative team approach, yet demonstrate top-down command decisions and a belief that prosocial behaviors can be coerced. They miss the mark because command leadership produces team compliance that merely acknowledges the positional power of the superintendent. A superintendent's ability to develop a team that achieves districtwide goals requires both the belief in collective competence and the skills to develop positive, prosocial attitudes.

DEVELOP AN AFFIRMATIVE ORIENTATION

Positive organizational scholarship is a well-researched theory that emphasizes human potential. The premise is that high-quality connections and positive emotions produce a collective capability that helps organizations thrive. The need to maintain amicable social relationships is important when people work closely together and coordinate activities. Work goes well and is experienced as pleasurable when relationships are attended to—and poorly when they are not (Shedd & Bacharach, 1991).

One of my principal colleagues is fond of saying, "Attitude: everyone has one. You may as well have a positive one." Every day he wears a little gold pin on his shirt collar that says "Attitude" as a reminder for all to stay the positive course even in the face of adversity and conflict.

Effective leaders have better-than-average interpersonal skills and build cooperative relationships with their followers. They are friendly, outgoing, responsive, encouraging, and diplomatic. They create attitudes among team members that become the foundation of successful teamwork. They praise others and their ideas, agreeing with and accepting the contribution of their colleagues (Keen, 2003).

LaFasto and Larson (2001) worked twenty years on research, followed by seven years of writing about a wide array of work teams. They found supportiveness to be an important factor in teamwork. In this context, a supportive team member would be someone who is easy to work with and who demonstrates a willingness to help others achieve goals. Another important teamwork factor that differentiated effective from ineffective team members is a positive personal style, characterized by enthusiasm about the work, getting along well with others, and being friendly and well liked. A strong positive attitude conveys affirmation of the worth of our fellow team members.

Thrive With the Positive

In the field of psychology, positive emotions are recognized as a factor that allows individuals and teams to thrive and flourish. Social scientists and psychologists have established an empirical research base and thus given credibility to why and how positive activities work to promote flourishing of both individuals and work groups (Cameron et al., 2003).

Think of the best seminar you have ever attended—that time when you learned a great deal and had fun doing it. In addition to providing relevant content, the seminar instructor likely sprinkled in humor, fun, ice breakers, and strategies to promote positive thoughts and actions. You were engaged. Likewise, a superintendent needs to be more like a good seminar instructor and less like the director of a stage play when meeting with the team of principals. If the superintendent is not comfortable leading these activities, then he or she should delegate this task to a team member who is comfortable in the role.

Positive emotions are worth cultivating because teams thrive in the presence of constructive experiences, supportive individual traits, and encouraging institutions (Cameron et al., 2003). Optimism, which is closely associated with the positive, is a cognitive process present when we expect a positive outcome. Optimists have high morale and feel upbeat and invigorated. They persevere, they hope. The superintendent begins to build optimism by demonstrating belief in the leadership capability of the principals, which in turn promotes the expectation of a positive result.

Play Together, Stay Together

When a focus is placed on the positive, a typical team meeting agenda looks a little different from a traditional meeting. Time for social interactions, play, and relationship activities are consistently built into the agenda, along with the more traditional reports, as the following example illustrates.

I asked a group of respected superintendent colleagues, including two who had been voted "State Superintendents of the Year," what they had on their agenda for the annual leadership team retreat at the beginning of the school year. On the typical agenda was a book study, a videotape of the latest learning theory, "start-up" information, and a problem or two to solve. What riveted my attention, though, was the discussion of activities not appearing on the printed agenda. These superintendents built in numerous opportunities for fun and energizing activities. They knew that, while educating students is challenging and the problems are serious, positive and fun team activities create the conditions that open minds to constructive problem solving. If staff development is not a significant part of your experience, search through books such as *Effective Group Facilitation in Education* (Eller, 2004) for ideas that can energize a team.

The Positive Principle

Groups as well as individuals benefit from the power of positive thoughts and actions. The power of affirmative experiences is widely accepted as providing personal benefits to an individual. Interestingly, groups also demonstrate a similar benefit when the positive process is applied. Specifically, the "broaden-and-build" theory (Fredrickson & Losada, 2005) recognizes that positive emotions broaden people's momentary thought-action repertoires and build their enduring personal resources, including the intellectual resources needed in leadership teams. Positive emotions widen our array of thoughts and actions, a great benefit when teams come together to solve problems. Positive effects also accumulate and compound over time, transforming people—and consequently teams—for the better. Teams become more socially integrated, knowledgeable, effective, and resilient. Evidence suggests that high ratios of positive to negative experiences will distinguish individuals who flourish from those who do not. These same principles have been successfully applied to teams. However, positive experiences may need to outnumber negative experiences at ratios appreciably higher than those typically demonstrated by many superintendents when working with a leadership team.

A Critical Ratio

You have probably heard motivational speakers talk about "making positive deposits to individuals' mental bank accounts." While this notion appeals to our experience and instinct, it is also based in science. In an experimental study, Fredrickson and Losada (2005) found that positive experiences need to outnumber the negative at a higher rate than previously believed to overcome the toxicity of the negative. Researchers found that a ratio of two times positive to one negative characterizes both individuals and teams that thrive and flourish. Reading this ratio reminded me of an elementary classroom I visited where the teacher taught the students how to make a "compliment sandwich" as a way to give constructive advice. She said, "Say something nice, then give your suggestion, then say something nice again."

Although simple, this advice illustrates that to function constructively and to flourish groups must experience a high rate of pleasant feelings. A caution is in order, however: The positive must be both appropriate and genuine or the leader risks losing credibility with the team. People sense when positive actions are feigned or forced. This kind of subterfuge will cause damage.

The superintendent brings out everyone's best by creating positive emotions when the team is together. Some specific positive strategies follow:

- Hold a quick drawing for small gift items to lift spirits.

- Ask principals to share a highlight of their week in the school.

- Place at each seat a small item such as notepad with the word "Attitude" on it.

- Take a break and engage in a brief energizing physical or mental activity.

- Use positive development strategies such as Appreciative Inquiry, discussed on page 11.

Appreciative Inquiry

Discovering the best of the human condition in organizations is fundamental to organizational development. One useful strategy is Appreciative Inquiry. Appreciative Inquiry (AI) can be defined as the art and practice of strengthening a system's capacity to heighten positive potential. AI is based on the assumption that teams or groups of people have a positive core that, when revealed and tapped, results in positive energy and positive improvement. This process involves identifying past examples of peak performances or spectacular successes. Key elements that account for these past successes are identified, and a vision of the future is crafted based on what was extraordinarily successful in the past and what can be perpetuated in the future (Cameron et al., 2003).

Appreciative Inquiry is based in large part on two decades of work by David Cooperrider (Salopek, 2006), who realized the power of questions that focus on successes. AI emphasizes cooperatively searching for and building on an organization's strengths and potential. It asks each team member to heighten awareness of the value of each person in the team. This asset-focused strategy works on the principle that positive questions lead to positive change, and that our words create our worlds (Markova & Holland, 2005). Practicing Appreciative Inquiry is a positive-thinking experience.

Relationships Rule

Work management, relationship management, and external boundary management are all necessary for a team to lead effectively in a demanding environment (Nadler & Spencer, 1998). Similarly, Glaser (2005) identified three important dimensions in team problem solving: relationships, content, and process. The common denominator between the work of Nadler, Spencer, and Glaser is relationships. Relationships are fundamental to all other work because they connect and link leaders. It is my experience and observation that, after completing a certification program, almost all principals and superintendents have mastered the content and tasks of the position. Despite their proficiency at the content and tasks, though, learning relationship management often takes time in the school of "hard knocks" as they learn the importance of peer and supervisory relationships.

As a first-year principal, I felt apprehensive when the superintendent asked me into his office one day. He was an experienced superintendent and cared about the inner workings of the leadership team. Gently he advised me to relax my task orientation. He assured me he had no doubt I knew the job content and was well prepared to handle the tasks of administration. He asked me to place equal importance on building relationships with the other principals by showing my positive, people-oriented social side.

"But," I protested, "I'm much younger than the other principals, a female, and less experienced. Won't they see me as naïve and weak?"

"No," he said, "they'll see you as human and approachable. They already know you have the skills because we hired you for the position. Now they need to know you as their friend and supportive colleague."

Like many new administrators, I had focused first on the content issues: Get the job done, raise the test scores, and check the items off the "to do" list. By habit, according to Glaser, we go straight to the content and forget about the importance of process and relationships. The reward from focusing on the positive is gaining a greater joy in the accomplishments of your leadership team.

TAKE-AWAY MESSAGE

Teamwork by itself is not sufficient to handle the complexities of positively impacting the achievement of all students, but without it a district becomes a collection of schools, not a team working toward common goals. The effective superintendent-principal leadership team works as diligently on relationship development as it does on test scores. In times of turmoil, affirmative leaders are needed to move teams forward and address the problems schools face. The knowledgeable superintendent assists principals to thrive and flourish by promoting high-quality connections and positive emotions between them.

CLOSING IN ON KEY CONCEPTS

- Teams are interdependent.
- Teams need to think "ours," not "my."
- Teams achieve their goals when each member envisions the desired team.
- Team values are elusive and lie deep beneath cosmetic behavior.
- Teams need to find ways to emphasize positive attitudes and to build healthy team emotions.
- Superintendents need sophisticated facilitative skills to form productive teams.

EXTENDING YOUR THINKING

1. It has been said that there is no "I" in team. What actions build the belief in "we" as opposed to "me"? How does a superintendent

communicate that the district's success is "ours" and a result of collective action? What inhibits or obstructs these beliefs from becoming a reality?

2. Is attitude really contagious? How can a team respond to a person who seems to be inoculated against a positive attitude?

3. Have you worked with a superintendent or supervisor who created joy and energy even when the team was doing the "tough stuff"? If yes, what contributed to this positive attitude? If no, what could have been done to make the work more welcome?

The Principal's Perspective

2

What Phenomenal Teams Look and Feel Like

> [O]rganizations . . . must create favorable conditions for people to spontaneously come together to share knowledge and learn as they explore organizational challenges.
>
> —Carol Beatty & Brenda Barker Scott (2004, p. 2)

When I think about the many school districts where I hired on as principal, it is easy to identify favorites. One in particular stands out. If Camelot is a "time, place, or atmosphere of idyllic happiness" (*Webster's*, 2003, p. 177), then this school district was the school administrators' version of Camelot.

What made this school district so extraordinary? Was the salary and benefit package exceptional? No, remuneration was below average for the region, and the number of required work days was well above. Could it have been the quality of the school I was assigned to? Certainly not! My new school was oversized and underachieving, came with a passel of personnel problems, and offered a facility long overdue for an upgrade. Nor was it the ease of the clientele—my school's middle class neighborhood was in deep transition. Immigrant families had begun to move in, bringing all the challenges associated with unfortunate poverty, dissimilar cultures, and a poor grasp of English.

When Shelly Harwayne (1999) wrote about the exacting work associated with starting up the Manhattan New School, she admonished educators to "choose their colleagues carefully" (p. 1). Harwayne's advice is well taken. In the school district where I toiled so joyfully, I had chosen wisely. It was my colleagues—especially the superintendent and principals—who made my new school district so special. These administrators were extraordinary to work with. Despite disparate backgrounds, personalities, talents, and professional experiences, together we made a phenomenal team.

TEAMWORK DEFINED

"Camelot" was led by Dr. Walt Bigby, a visionary superintendent supported by one highly competent assistant, several energetic program directors, and eight fervent principals. The membership of this team was just large enough to make communication difficult, ambitious enough to generate a plethora of projects, and opinionated enough to make teamwork something to be worked at. Yet these administrators personified the word "teamwork"; they coalesced around important goals, tackled the challenges at hand, and accomplished wonders.

What do we mean by teamwork, that elusive interpersonal concept that organizations struggle to attain and so often fail to achieve? The definition crafted by Beatty and Barker Scott (2004) cuts to the core: "By teamwork, we mean *real* teamwork, whereby the right people with the right skills, knowledge, and perspective join to collectively explore challenges, generate creative solutions, and work diligently to build the necessary support and commitment for implementation" (p. 2, italics mine). My favorite school district had the right people, doing the right work, in the right way. Problems were acknowledged and important goals set; solutions were identified and plans implemented with success. How lucky I was to be a part of it!

THE RIGHT PEOPLE

When it came to hiring principals, Walt was particular. He sought kindred spirits—enthusiastic administrators, well grounded in pedagogy, and passionate about improving schools—and he took the extra steps needed to find them. I was startled to get a call from Walt himself shortly after I submitted his district's lengthy application for a principal position. Before selecting me for an interview, he wanted to know more: What were my beliefs about developmentally appropriate practices? How did I set goals for my school? Where would I be in five years? Thirty minutes later I had the interview scheduled, but, more important, I had learned that selective administrators take care when choosing members for their teams.

Why You Need Them

School leaders fighting the reform war—and the barrage of state and federal "accountability" mandates that accompany this battle—need a platoon of highly effective people to march forward. There is nothing more frustrating for supervisors, or a greater obstacle to success, than incompetent team members. Fullan (2003) cautioned school administrators to be realistic about purposeful, sustainable school reform; it is definitely not a one-man show. He urges administrators to build highly skilled, self-directed, forward-moving teams. At the same time, though, Fullan wryly observes "the biggest dilemma facing all leaders . . . is what to do if you *don't* trust the competence and motivation of the people you are expected to lead (p. 66, italics mine). Fullan's observation will resonate with the many school administrators across this country whose success is thwarted daily by ineffectual employees.

Not surprisingly, competent team members are a precursor to success in the corporate world. But what *is* surprising is that CEOs of high-performing companies choose the right people before choosing the right project. In *Good to Great,* Collins's book that details how good companies become extraordinary companies (Collins, 2001), Collins likened the recruitment of outstanding team members to getting the right people on the bus. What difference does this make? "[I]f you have the right people . . . the problem of how to motivate and manage people largely goes away. The right people don't need to be tightly managed or fired up; they will be self motivated by the inner drive to produce the best results and to be part of creating something great" (Collins, p. 42).

SUCCESS WITH INTACT TEAMS

What if there is no opportunity to choose the right person for your team? In most cases, a superintendent moving into a new a district will find the administrative team already in place. Superintendents inheriting intact principal teams must make relationship building a top priority. This involves clear expectations and strong communication. Our book presents strategies for both of these in Chapters 5 and 6, respectively. Perfecting the performances of individual principals and the superintendent-principal team are also vital steps. These responsibilities are thoroughly addressed in Chapters 7 and 8. With the right strategies, a superintendent's relationship with an "intact" team will be an unqualified success.

How to Get Them

When I arrived for my interview in what would become my favorite school district, the usual candidate-screening games were conspicuously absent. No tasks to be sorted into priority piles, letters to write to cranky patrons, or simulated committee meetings to run. My selection would hinge solely on a lengthy discussion with a multidisciplinary team, an exhaustive review of my professional accomplishments, and meticulous reference checking.

————————————— ❦ —————————————

THE HEART AND SOUL OF THE MATTER

Looking for a sterling principal? Take note of the following hiring essentials:

• Hire early. Recruit early to attract the best candidates. To avoid "late hires," some districts use a "rolling timeline" that includes advertising for new positions in the preceding fall. Learn about this and other innovative practices by accessing the research report "Improved Principal Hiring: Findings and Recommendations for Urban Schools" (The New Teacher Project [TNTP], 2006) on line.

• Know what you want. Are you looking for an instructional leader, school climate builder, a no-nonsense disciplinarian, or all of these and more? Sourcebooks such as *Standards for What Principals Should Know and Be Able to Do* (National Association of Elementary School Principals [NAESP], 2001) and the *Standards for School Leaders* (Council of Chief State School Officers [CCSSO], 1996) will help you pinpoint your priorities. Just be sure to align application, screening, and interview materials to selected job specifications.

• Put your best foot forward. Attractive position announcements, enticing school brochures, and professional-looking application packets communicate confidence in your school district. Include helpful information about your community as well, such as maps, a current local newspaper, and chamber of commerce brochures.

• Educate application screeners. Sometimes inexperienced screeners unwittingly reject highly desirable candidates. They ax the well educated for being "overqualified," those with nontraditional backgrounds for being "bad fits," and applicants who have successfully worked in a variety of communities for "moving around too much." Make certain your screeners know job specifications, how to recognize "hotshots," and when to flex criteria to draw in sterling, albeit unorthodox, candidates.

• Ask tough questions. Avoid interview questions that are so open ended any answer will do. Ask questions such as, "What are six research-supported instructional practices in reading?" or ask the candidate to "Name five promising trends in education today." Include response criteria for each question so that interviewers know what to look for and how to score responses.

• Involve decision makers in every activity. If you require applicants to make presentations, give postobservation feedback to teachers, or participate in meeting simulations, make certain that the people making the final hiring decision witness every activity. Otherwise, decision makers will not be able to fairly appraise each candidate's capabilities.

• Spend quality time with the finalists. I am still perplexed by the personnel secretary who handed me a timer at the start of an interview with instructions to limit my responses to a couple of minutes per question. I was sternly warned not to go over time. Does this make sense? A wisely handled interview reveals "the heart and soul" of each applicant, so schedule sufficient time.

- Check references ruthlessly. Conduct in-depth reference checks with all former supervisors. Ask questions about instructional leadership; support for students, staff, and clients; and management of funds and resources. Look for congruency between interview impressions and reference reports.

- Be there. Are you a superintendent? Then be there for the interview and help your team identify the best principal for the school district.

I was impressed to learn that Walt was part of the interview team. Incredulously, even though principals are the ones superintendents most depend on to make their visions a reality, there are superintendents who delegate principal selection to assistants. I survived the interview, got the job, and went to work. The next few years would become the most exhilarating of my career.

THE RIGHT WORK

I soon learned that student achievement throughout the district had begun to slip after years of reliable growth. At the bottom of the academic heap were newly arrived migrant students whose lack of English, transient life styles, and academic deficits not only were barriers to success, but also placed alarming demands on their ill-prepared teachers. Next up were at-risk students from impoverished, English-speaking families whose numbers had skyrocketed due to the recent influx of low-income apartments. At the top were "advantaged" students from middle-income families whose lackluster test scores revealed they were coasting.

Despite an abundance of progressive projects and a huge investment in technology, our schools were keeping pace neither with changing demographics nor our state department of education's heightened focus on accountability. Students were expected to meet state standards: end of story. Our students were not, and the magnitude of the underlying problems was breathtaking: underperforming students at all socioeconomic levels, language challenges among students most at risk, inadequately prepared teachers, and an ineffective curricular approach from elementary through secondary. Nevertheless, my superintendent moved forward with remarkable confidence. When Collins (2001) studied men and women who faced alarming obstacles, he identified an intriguing dichotomy: "It didn't matter how bleak the situation or how stultifying their mediocrity, they all maintained unwavering faith that they would . . . prevail" (p. 87).

Under Walt's reassuring leadership, we set a single but substantive goal: to raise student achievement in core subjects. We analyzed data and identified weaknesses, researched best practices and learned new teaching strategies, adopted new instructional programs and helped teachers implement them. Nothing startling, you might think. Isn't this the normal path superintendents take to raise student test scores? But there was a difference.

THE RIGHT WAY

The principals and district administrators demonstrated a Herculean work ethic and an enduring esprit de corps as they embraced the multitude of tasks that might have paralyzed a weaker team. Despite the typical problems associated with change—time constraints, reluctant teachers, suspicious unions, shoestring budgets—everyone worked enthusiastically, collaboratively, and competently.

The work, although demanding, seemed totally effortless. And the mission, although daunting, seemed completely doable. Why? Looking back with decades of management experience behind me, I know now that it was Walt's keen leadership that kept his team from faltering. His tactics might seem unexceptional, but our success lay not in the novelty of his approach, but in its execution. My superintendent skillfully led his team by setting the stage, narrowing the agenda, leading fearlessly, radiating optimism, supporting, affirming, and "being there."

Setting the Stage

Walt was a soft-spoken individual who articulated his vision with conviction but without fanfare. Few administrators are or need be charismatic. In fact, grandiose personalities are *negatively* correlated with successful leadership (Collins, 2001). Walt was persuasive because his mission made sense. It didn't spring from the polemic of a popular guru or the latest fad, but from the unmistakable problems at hand.

After bringing his administrative team on board, Walt directly reached out to teachers and support staff, delivering his message, without intermediary. His personal approach, coupled with hard data, helped staff grasp the need for reform. Although Walt was fervent about improving achievement, he was wise enough not to orchestrate every move; he directed his principals and teachers to craft the improvement plans for their schools. We felt responsible and valued.

What is a good leader? Perhaps it is nothing more than someone people want to follow. We were eager to follow our superintendent because his vision was compelling and he had earned our trust. What's more, Walt cemented our commitment by trusting us in return.

Narrowing the Agenda

It is de rigueur for school goal plans to address not only student achievement, but also an alphabet soup of related concerns—staff morale, parent education, school safety, discipline, technology, and community involvement, to name just a few. Typically, each issue requires one or more goals, each goal is supported by an array of objectives, and each objective is accompanied by a lengthy list of activities with detailed timelines. The better plans include how student achievement will be measured (e.g., administering reading fluency tests), and how activity completion will be documented (e.g., taking roll to verify program participation). Not surprisingly, school goal plans are tedious to prepare and become hefty tomes few staff members read and even fewer believe will be completed. In his trend-setting book, *Renewing America's Schools,* Carl Glickman (1993) linked the failure of schools to improve to overwrought, ill-defined goals: "Unfortunately, part of the reason why schools are such easy targets for criticism is that their goals are so diffuse and fragmented. We read that schools should have goals that address basic skills, self-esteem, vocational skills, higher order thinking, health and nutrition, character education, responsible and cooperative behavior, aesthetic appreciation, and so on. With such diffuse goals, it is obvious that schools will not do well on some" (p. 7). In contrast, successful school districts have a "laser like focus on teaching and learning" (Fullan, 2005, p. 68), which in my new school district emanated from the superintendent. Since student achievement was Walt's sole goal, that goal became the focus of our school improvement plans. Our teachers targeted reading, writing, and math for improvement; their interventions focused on classroom instructional practices. Student success was measured through periodic progress monitoring and annual state assessment results. Because the superintendent had narrowed the agenda to the critical few, our school improvement plans were substantive yet simple. Teachers and administrators knew the goals and had confidence in their capacity to attain them.

Leading Fearlessly

Once a week, Walt gathered his administrative team for a lengthy, early morning breakfast meeting. The agenda—departmental briefings, school progress reports, budget updates, data reviews, legislative recaps—was unremarkable. What *was* remarkable, though, was the superintendent's expectation for his team. Walt wanted hard data, frank appraisals, and tough questions. Sound easy? Hardly!

> The rare chief executive who *truly* wants to know what's going on at the point of delivery soon learns they can't break through. The general atmosphere of blame and fear that grows up over the years in our organizations discourages the passage of unadulterated data up through the organization, especially if there are undertones of failure. Heads roll when things go wrong, and no one wants to be associated with bad news. So, good data gets multiplied many times as it begins its way up, and bad data is played down or covered up. Ultimately, it means that those on the strategic decision-making level can't learn about themselves and their performance. They are operating in the dark, sometimes practically blind. (Dolan, 1994, p. 33, italics mine)

Our superintendent was not afraid of bad news, and his principals learned they could share problems without penalty. If a school's achievement scores dropped, for example, the setback was discussed by the team, and the principal of that school received offers of support. The risk-free environment that Walt created fostered open communication and precipitated fierce debates about everything under the educational sun: collaborative versus traditional bargaining, phonics versus whole language, language immersion versus bilingual instruction, and site-based versus centralized decision making. The frank talk was invigorating for the administrative team and provided our superintendent with the information he needed.

Radiating Optimism

Effective leaders are affective leaders. They know the significance attitude has on the people they direct. The authors of *Primal Leadership* (Goleman, Boyatzis, & McKee, 2002) affirmed this approach: "The fundamental task of leaders, we argue, is to prime good feeling in those they lead. That occurs when a leader creates resonance—a reservoir of positivity that frees the best in people" (p. ix).

Walt's "reservoir of positivity" was wide and deep. He nurtured "good feeling" by being unfailingly upbeat. When presented with a thorny problem he would say, "We'll fix that." When setbacks were encountered, he would ask, "How else can we go about doing this?" Walt pursued his goals relentlessly, and his principals eagerly followed in his footsteps. We believed we could accomplish anything because our boss believed this of us, unequivocally.

A bonus was Walt's gentle sense of humor. He told jokes at his own expense, laughed at problems that seemed insurmountable, and poked fun when spirits wavered. And if mistakes were made and the atmosphere became tense, he would take the edge off by finding something amusing about the predicament we were in. Laughter reduces anxiety, softens disaccord, and provides a shared experience that pulls people together and frees them to do their best work. Lindle (2005) put it this way: "Solutions often start with humor. Just as scarcity is the mother of invention, humor drives creativity. Humor cements relationships and opens up imagination" (p. 27). With optimism and a healthy dose of humor, Walt energized team performance.

Supporting

Fullan (2005) has written extensively about developing the capacity of educators to lead schools. He advocates a team approach: "Capacity building involves developing the *collective ability*—dispositions, skills, knowledge, motivation, and resources—to act together to bring about positive change" (p. 4, italics mine). But building capacity needs more than a firm belief in this vital concept: it also takes time, training, and resources, which requires money. In my own school, I needed to bring in substitute teachers so teachers could observe master-level colleagues, to find consultants who would help us inspire unmotivated children, and to put research-supported reading materials into the hands of teachers. Although funds were scarce, Walt allocated discretionary monies to each school so that principals could bring school improvement plans to fruition. Training was also provided on pertinent topics such as organizational change, curricular alignment, intentional instructional strategies, and classroom-based assessments. Getting needed resources and training accelerated momentum and rapidly moved us forward.

Affirming

One day Walt unexpectedly charged into my office excitedly waving a fist full of documents. He had just received our school district's self-study results and my school had performed well. Walt had come to congratulate my staff in person. I will long remember this personal touch. Following his lead, when there is good news to deliver in my own school, I do it in person.

❦

THE RIGHT WAY

Setting the Stage

Credible vision

Reaching out

Team trust

Narrowing the Agenda

Teaching and learning

The "critical few"

Leading Fearlessly

Eliciting bad news

Risk-free environment

Radiating Optimism

Humor

Modeling

Supporting

Training and resources

Funding

Affirming

Person to person

Quality work

Being There

Participating

Leading

There were other ways Walt let us know that our work was valued. Principals who produced something he liked—an illuminating test score analysis, a unique curricular guide—were asked to share it at a team meeting. And if an award had been won, a grant snagged, or an article published, Walt highlighted these successes in district newsletters and at board meetings. Most coveted, however, were his invitations to represent the district at an important conference, or to join one of his "task force" committees. Affirmation inspires us to go above and beyond. Like that soul-stirring Olympic slogan, my superintendent knew how to "light the fire within" (International Olympic Committee, 2002).

Being There

Roland Barth (2003) warned school leaders, "If you want to have your say, you've got to be present for the conversation" (p. 23). What does this look like for a superintendent? Walt led our weekly business meetings and additional "school improvement" work sessions. He orchestrated administrative inservices, summer retreats, and trips to workshops and conferences. And yes, he participated in each of these activities. Walt also talked to principals about their goals, read our school newsletters, dropped by our schools, and personally reviewed student achievement results. There is an old saying about making connections: "If you don't have a relationship, you don't have a relationship." My superintendent made certain that he had a relationship with his principals by "being there."

TAKE-AWAY MESSAGE

Principals benefit from a job culture that inspires, directs, and supports. Effective superintendents provide vision, set the tone for team interactions, and model success strategies for their principals. When superintendents "create favorable conditions" (Beatty & Barker Scott, 2004, p. 2) and develop an empowering team environment, principals flourish!

CLOSING IN ON KEY CONCEPTS

- Take care when choosing the members of your team.
- Do the right work in the right way.
- Face challenges with optimism.
- Create a credible vision, then trust your team to bring it to life.
- Keep goal plans simple.
- Create a fearless work place.
- Nurture good feelings; affirm quality work.
- Provide support—fund initiatives, provide training, and be there.
- Create a phenomenal team by being a phenomenal team member.

EXTENDING YOUR THINKING

1. What do the right people—teacher, principal, district administrators—look like in your organization? How do you get them on board?

2. Can the members of your administrative team express opinions openly and freely? Why or why not? How do team members react when "bad news" is delivered?

3. Do you work with colleagues who face challenges with optimism? Does this positive attitude affect your own perceptions of problems? How do you "lift" the spirits of your team members?

4. When was the last time someone expressed appreciation for your work? How do you affirm the people you work with?

PART II

Leadership Qualities

In Part II, the impact of leadership qualities is examined. Chapter 3 reveals what superintendents really want in a principal. It uses the notion of "triple bottom line" to convey the attributes today's principals need for success. Chapter 4 identifies the characteristics of superlative superintendents and their connection to strong principal performance.

The Superintendent's Perspective

3

What Superintendents Want in a Principal

All individuals, teams, and organizations that have achieved greatness accomplished this only with the vast waves of motivational power released when passion was tapped and renewed on a continual basis.

—Robert E. Staub (2001, p. 3)

A popular poster a few years ago depicted a principal dressed as Superman. The poster, tongue in cheek, listed all the numerous competencies a principal should possess, including the ability to change the course of mighty rivers and leap tall buildings in a single bound. Today's poster may look more like an ad in the personals section of the classifieds:

Superintendent Seeking Superprincipal. Wanted: a man or woman with the character of Abraham Lincoln, the educational mind of John Dewey, the personality of Dale Carnegie, and the heart of Mother Teresa.

Although this ad is a spoof and product of my imagination, it may be close to the truth. I have many opportunities to dialogue with various groups of superintendents through my work, both as a superintendent and as an instructor of future superintendents. At a recent superintendents meeting, I asked what qualities and skills these school CEO's expect in a principal. Superintendents in attendance quickly agreed that a principal needs to be competent, caring, committed, demonstrate a strong work ethic, and possess a wide array of positive personal characteristics and communication skills. No matter the length of the list, the Number 1 response was always the expectation that the principal will positively impact student achievement as measured by test scores.

Test scores are the high-stakes measurement that has become the schools' business equivalent of bottom-line profitability. However, today's most successful companies do care about more than just profit. Consider the coffee company Starbucks. Starbucks began as a small Seattle coffee bean retailer in 1987. It is now an international business, and boasts the world's largest chain of coffee shops. The key to their success is their promotion of a triple bottom line (Michelli, 2007). Naturally, Starbucks' leaders must report financial results. Less to be expected, they must also report the social impact and environmental performance of their work. These findings are published in the annual Corporate Social Responsibility Report as a result of an annual independently conducted audit. An abbreviated version is available in Starbucks' stores for customers. Superintendents, I propose, also have a triple bottom line for considering the performance of principals. Whether or not reported in a written report, the triple bottom line for principals is competence, character, and a caring heart.

COMPETENCE

Superintendents I talked with consistently described the following three essential attributes as defining competence for principals: skill in instructional leadership, evidence of continuous learning, and the ability to manage the change process. Let's look more closely at what each indicator of competence might look like, and describe some steps that principals can take toward mastery of the three components.

Skill in Instructional Leadership

Superintendents in my sample defined instructional leadership as a set of skills that impact teachers and, consequently, student learning. These skills also include a combination of group process strategies and data analysis ability. Superintendents value teamwork, especially collaboration and staff participation in principals' decision making. Principals are also expected to use and analyze a wide range of data, including test scores, dropout and behavior statistics, and staff and community surveys. A superintendent I know summed up one of the group discussions I held this way: "The focus of a school *must* be on student learning. The principal should expect effective instruction and monitor the effectiveness of instruction and its impact on student learning." This expectation articulated by superintendents is supported in a survey conducted by McEwan (2003). While educators might not always be clear about the definition of instruction leadership, they are very clear on its importance (McEwan).

The principal historically is the principal teacher. Thus, principal leadership is evidenced through increases in the professional development of teachers. Teachers in a study reported two major dimensions of effective instructional leadership as the most effective principal behaviors: the ability to cause teachers to reflect on practice, and encouragement of professional growth (Blase & Blase, 2000). Principals promote professional growth through collaborative dialogue, using vehicles such as peer coaching, collegial study groups, and reflective discussions.

Becoming an exemplary instructional leader is a never-ending learning journey. Ensuring quality instruction is fundamental to the principal's work. Selected readings that provide additional reflections and insight regarding the role of instructional leader are found in the box.

SUGGESTED READINGS ON INSTRUCTIONAL LEADERSHIP

Handbook of Instructional Leadership by Jo Blase and Joseph Blase (1998)

Professional Learning Communities at Work by Richard DuFour and Robert Eaker (1998)

Getting Excited About Data by Edie Holcomb (1999)

Making Schools Smarter by Kenneth Leithwood, Robert Aitken, and Doris Jantzi (2006)

School Leadership That Works: From Research to Results by Robert Marzano, Timothy Waters, and Brian McNulty (2005)

10 Traits of Highly Effective Principals: From Good to Great Performance by Elaine McEwan (2003)

Results NOW by Mike Schmoker (2006)

The Principalship: A Reflective Practice Perspective by Thomas Sergiovani (1987)

Evidence of Continuous Learning

In any organization, employers seek people with a passion for self-improvement, those who take responsibility for their own personal and professional development, and those who are willing to acquire expertise that adds value to the organization (Macpherson & Finch, 2006). Nowhere is this continuous learning more imperative than in the demanding environment of today's schools. Superintendents expect principals to keep learning throughout their careers.

Every principal I have met believes he or she works hard—very hard. I have had the chance to stand in the shoes of both principal and superintendent. I've seen firsthand that the principalship is the most demanding job in today's educational environment. Change is rapid and constant. Today's higher expectations require more skills and understanding than ever before. Principals are expected to maintain the traditional job of management, and to add the leadership qualities necessary for instructional improvement. Moreover, principals must skillfully work through the teachers, and motivate them to grow continuously. Thus, to lead and inspire staff, principals too must be continuous learners and must take responsibility for their own professional growth.

Continuous professional growth requires a deep knowledge of content and a wide array of skills acquired through reading, engaging in conferences and workshops, and networking with colleagues. Another way to develop the capacity to think outside the box is by taking advantage of reading material outside the field of education. Connecting ideas between education and other fields stimulates creative thinking and deep reflection.

We often hear "there is no money" for professional development, but that is not true: resources for lifelong learning are everywhere. Not all principals have budgets that support travel across the United States to a conference or workshop, but all principals are expected to do more than the traditional job. Continually ask yourself and your superintendent, "How can I improve?" After targeting growth areas, take advantage of free or inexpensive ideas for continuous learning. It takes fifteen minutes to complain about lack of resources. Instead, use those minutes to read something that motivates, teaches, or inspires you to go the extra mile. Resources are everywhere and many of them cost only the time you set aside to take advantage of them.

Superintendents will assist principals to learn, but principals should not expect superintendents to provide all of the training or guidance. As one superintendent told me, "I expect to take principals from a bud to a flower. I don't expect to grow them from a seed." Commit to your own learning.

SUGGESTED STRATEGIES FOR INEXPENSIVE PROFESSIONAL GROWTH

Read outside of education. For instance, take a look at the *Harvard Business Review* or *The New Yorker*.

Use your local library. Books on business, community, and religious leaders can be inspirational.

Surf educational sites on the Internet. Learn to use new technology.

Attend a motivational seminar with a friend or colleague so you can debrief and discuss ideas after the event.

Network with exemplary colleagues and discuss educational or political issues.

Attend a lecture given by a noneducator. Such lectures are frequently free of charge at community colleges, local libraries, or book stores.

Browse the local bookstore for interesting new topics and authors.

Think of something you enjoyed learning in high school or college and follow up with it. For instance, if you learned a foreign language in college, listen to a CD or radio station in that language while driving to and from work.

Managing the Change Process

Count the number of topics and books on the topic of "change" that have been published or reported on at conferences in recent years. The popularity of the topic indicates that it is an enormous concern and an important process for the principal to manage. Change would be easy if it were merely a matter of implementing standards or analyzing data or developing a plan. But in the principal's world, change means challenge—challenge to the status quo, challenge to teachers' traditional classroom autonomy, challenge to our ability to persuade people and to handle the inevitable conflicts that result. It has been said that nobody likes change but a wet baby. That may be true, but change is inherent in all we do as school leaders. If you don't learn to manage change, you could become a casualty of another adage—the one where the baby gets tossed out with the bath water.

Waters, Marzano, and McNulty (2003) wrote in *Balanced Leadership: What 30 Years of Research Tells Us About the Effect of Leadership on Student Achievement* that flexibility is the most important of the effective leadership practices. When some think of flexibility they think of indecisiveness or going along to get along, neither of which is necessarily part of flexibility. Flexibility is the ability to adapt leadership behaviors to the needs of the current situation. "Many principals cannot adapt to change or think on their feet," says a veteran superintendent when discussing problematic principal behaviors.

Flexibility also means being comfortable with dissent and developing skills in managing conflict-resolution skills, facilitating difficult conversations, and responding to shifting priorities. Today's educational environment is about change. Those who embrace it will thrive and those who resist it will not.

SUGGESTED READINGS ON CHANGE

The New Meaning of Educational Change by Michael Fullan (2001)

School Leadership That Works: From Research to Results by Robert Marzano, Timothy Waters, and Brian McNulty (2005)

Leading Effective Secondary School Reform by Mikie Loughridge and Loren Tarantino (2005)

How Schools Change by Tony Wagner (2000)

How to Deal With Teachers Who Are Angry, Troubled, Exhausted, or Just Plain Confused by Elaine McEwan (2005)

The Principal as Professional Development Leader by Phyllis Lindstrom and Marsha Speck (2004)

CHARACTER

Character, according to *Webster's* (2003, p. 207), is the "complex of mental and ethical traits marking and . . . individualizing a person." Character, according to most superintendents, is a demonstration of certain preferred behaviors. Superintendents in my sample group most frequently listed preferred principal behaviors as being integrity and courage, a strong work ethic, and a commitment to communicate.

Integrity and Courage

Writing in the *Journal for Quality and Participation*, Staub (2001) placed integrity above all other qualities that are important for effective leaders. All of the competencies in the world will not serve an enterprise or leader if there is a lack of integrity in the leadership effort. Integrity implies more than simply being honest and truthful: it also implies the courage to consistently and truly match actions to words. It is exemplified in the popular phrase, "If you're going to talk the talk, you've got to walk the walk." One superintendent offered this advice to principals:

"Tell the truth even if it challenges the status quo or ruffles feathers. Even when the journey gets rough, if you are willing to tell the truth others learn to trust you."

A Strong Work Ethic

When superintendents discuss ethics, they focus on the importance of a strong work ethic. We have all read about the leisure ethic; superintendents still adhere to the traditional work ethic. These district leaders define a strong work ethic as the tenacity and perseverance to work hard and the dedication to achieve success. They support the notion that going above and beyond, not doing just enough to get by, is required for today's principals. They expect principals to make their schools their top priority. These superintendents know that good is not good enough to demonstrate commitment to the work.

A Commitment to Communicate

All superintendents in my discussion group agree that it is critically important that they be kept informed. Moreover, it is far better to *over-inform* than to *under*inform the superintendent. School and district leaders live in a fishbowl; local news and information is easily accessible to all. Moreover, the media seem to thrive on, and give exceptional attention to, outrageous stories.

Keep in mind that communications flow both ways. I recollect a principal coming to me with a concern. "I made a bad decision," he said, and then told me the story. (The details remain confidential to protect his identity.) It was definitely a story that could have ended badly. I was surprised at his lapse in personal and professional judgment, but I put that feeling aside in order to solve the problem. We were able to both talk and listen to each other. As a result, we eventually unraveled the legal implications through an attorney and informed the school board of this potentially embarrassing situation. This principal and I both learned that early communication can prevent problems and protect both the superintendent and the principal.

"How will I know how much to communicate?" a new principal once asked me. He indicated that he was concerned about running to the superintendent with every inconsequential matter. The advice to principals from superintendents is, "Trust your instincts." "Those 'red flag' signs should not be ignored," advised a superintendent. A brief description of the concern is usually sufficient to communicate. "Give me the short version; I'll ask if I need more," one superintendent advised principals.

Know what's going on in your school and in your district. Listen to kids on the bus, in casual conversations, or in the hallways. Kids often know when something is amiss. Read the local paper. Subscribe to a state or regional news-clipping service and watch for indicators of potential problems heading your way. What happens in one district generally shows up in another district eventually. If you find yourself in a public situation regarding a matter that you had thought was private, be honest and communicate quickly. Then advise the superintendent, who will look at the facts and advise you appropriately. Very little is private any more (Avolio, Kahai, & Dodge, 2000). This lack of privacy has increased the need for timely, frequent, and transparent communication.

A CARING HEART

Superintendents talk about caring as a fundamental attribute sought in a principal. They describe caring as a focus on students but also as a positive attitude and a set of well-honed interpersonal skills. The following examples illustrate this point.

Care About Kids

All superintendents I talked with agree that the love of children is a number one quality sought in a principal. One superintendent speaking to my class of principal interns summed it up by saying, "You've got to have a heart for kids, like and enjoy them, believe in them, make them the focus of your work." Moreover, another district leader continued, "Caring should extend to *all* children in the school, including those with special needs, the gifted, the average, the troubled." Yet another added, "We can teach principals the school district procedures. What we look for is a caring heart and a genuine love of kids."

Care About Your Attitude

Attitudes convey values and beliefs. Take care so that your actions and words portray a belief in teamwork and a "can do" attitude. A superintendent describes it this way. "I want a principal to think that this school and this district are the best place in the world. Instead of thinking 'poor us, poor me,' which seems to be rampant in today's high-stakes, high-pressure-cooker schools, I like the 'cup is half full' orientation." Think positive. Even if it does not change the outcome, it certainly changes others' perceptions of your attitude.

Care About Your Interpersonal Skills

Experienced school leaders know that the job is highly interpersonal in nature. To interact successfully with the various school stakeholders requires a high degree of skill. Specifically, five behaviors account for up to 25 percent of the variance in leadership ability (Smith & Canger, 2004). Smith and Canger conducted a meta-analysis of interpersonal behaviors called the "Big Five" framework. The Big Five interpersonal leadership behaviors are (1) emotional stability, (2) extraversion, (3) openness, (4) agreeableness, and (5) conscientiousness. Moreover, they found compelling evidence that the supervisor's personality and ability in these interpersonal skills influence the attitudes of the staff. Staff evidenced a more positive job-related attitude when the supervisor had higher levels of the Big Five attributes. The researchers conclude that agreeable individuals tend to be more trusting of others and to be better team players. Emotionally stable individuals have a lower threshold of anxiety, hostility, and depression, thus are less likely to exhibit intimidating behaviors such as losing their temper. Only one caution was revealed: overly conscientious supervisors, although dependable and achievement oriented, tend to be overbearing and "nit picky." If you have a tendency to be overly conscientious, then plentiful quantities of the other four attributes are needed to overcome a potential negative image.

TAKE-AWAY MESSAGE

Learn to lead wholeheartedly (Staub, 2001). Principals and superintendents who lead wholeheartedly use a set of powerful communication practices and exhibit values associated with a strong character. The entire being of a leader is required to show up for work each day. This is a highly demanding way of working and relating and is not for the dilettante school or district leaders. Required is character, commitment, interpersonal skills, and a genuine care for students. Preferred are demonstrations of daily acts of courage. The chapter began with an ad for Superprincipal. If this describes you, apply today. Compensation is commensurate to your personal investment.

CLOSING IN ON KEY CONCEPTS

- Instructional leadership and interpersonal skills are necessary ingredients of a valued principal.
- Exemplary principals must be continuous learners to keep up with the demands of reform and change.

- Superintendents value principals who demonstrate integrity and courage, a strong work ethic, and a commitment to communicate.
- Trusted principals personally communicate both the good and the bad news, and thus assist the superintendent to manage the media.
- Principals care about kids as well as about their own attitude and interpersonal skills.

EXTENDING YOUR THINKING

1. Personally reflect on your attitude and actions that affect the superintendent-principal team. Do you view your cup as half full? Would your team members agree with your self-evaluation?

2. How can leaders balance their personal and professional demands so that the entire heart and mind are engaged in educational issues when on the job?

3. What are three things you can do today to be the exemplary principal your superintendent would wish to honor with a "lifetime contract"? What three things would you recommend to others to be that exemplary leader?

The Principal's Perspective

4

Superintendents Principals Want to Work For

Visionary leadership is knowing how to inspire hearts, ignite minds, and move hands to create tomorrow.

—John R. Hoyle, Lars G. Björk,
Virginia Collier, & Thomas E. Glass (2005, p. 21)

I have had the unique opportunity to work for more than a dozen superintendents over the course of my long career. I have witnessed performance levels ranging from substandard to superlative, and just about every level in between. Without a doubt, I would follow the superlative superintendent to the ends of this earth. What makes a superintendent extraordinary?

Identifying the quintessential attributes of a high-quality superintendent is no easy task. There is a dearth of research devoted solely to the qualities of the superintendent, so one has to be guided by the volumes of research on leadership. Here, though, we might find that there is too much information, which is as perplexing as too little. When it comes to leadership, there are countless theories, opposing ideas, and conflicting experiences. Northouse sums up the dilemma succinctly: "Some researchers conceptualize leadership as a trait, or as a behavior, while others view leadership from a political perspective, or from a humanistic viewpoint. Leadership has been studied using both qualitative and quantitative methods in many contexts. . . . Collectively, the research findings on leadership . . . provide a picture of a process that is *far* more sophisticated and complex than the often simplistic view presented in some of the popular books" (Northouse, 2007, italics mine).

To complicate matters, what rookie principals need from their superintendent differs from what veteran principals need, as I saw when I surveyed my colleagues. Kari Henderson-Burke, a bright, newly minted elementary administrator, hopes for a supportive boss who will, in her words, "process a situation with me and help me learn from my mistakes." Eric Cahan, another fresh-from-the-box principal with a demanding— and exhausting—high school assignment, wants a supervisor whose "caring for the principal as a *person* is job one." In contrast, Dick Panagos, a confident, well-seasoned middle school manager, looks foremost for a boss who exudes "candor and trust." As for me, I appreciate a superintendent who knows my work well enough to trust my intuitive—and at times unorthodox—approach to school management. Although our needs vary, there is a critical attribute that frames our pictures of the perfect superintendent—we all want a secure relationship with our boss.

THE TRANSFORMATIONAL LEADER

There are several decades' worth of research on transformational leadership, an intriguing concept Northouse expertly summarizes in his definitive book *Leadership: Theory and Practice*: "[T]ransformational leadership is concerned with the *process* of how certain leaders are able to inspire followers to accomplish great things. This approach stresses that leaders need to understand and adapt to the needs and motives of followers. Transformational leaders are recognized as change agents who are good role models, who can create and articulate clear vision for an organization, who empower followers to achieve at higher standards, and who act in ways that make others want to trust them, and who give meaning to organizational life" (Northouse, 2007, p. 198, italics mine). The characteristics of transformational leadership affirmed my own experiences: the superintendents I treasure communicate a crystal-clear vision, and have a knack for building enduring, trusting relationships with their principals.

EMOTIONALLY INTELLIGENT LEADERSHIP

In *Primal Leadership*, Goleman and colleagues (2002) took the "transformational leadership" concept farther by linking it to new information about how the human body reacts to influences in the work environment: "Breakthroughs in brain research show why leaders' moods and actions have enormous impact on those they lead, and shed fresh light on the power of emotionally intelligent leadership to inspire, arouse passion and enthusiasm, and keep people motivated and committed" (p. ix).

Extensive investigations by the authors of *Primal Leadership* led them to the interpersonal traits of highly successful leaders—tagged "EI" for "emotionally intelligent" (Goleman et al., 2002, p. 20). These leaders are knowledgeable about how their organizations operate, are sensitive to the concerns and opinions of others, and work actively to meet the needs of the people they serve. These savvy leaders are experts with relationships: they inspire others, enhance the performance of their subordinates, step up to the plate when change is needed, and collaborate with the members of their team (Goleman et al.).

SUPERLATIVE SUPERINTENDENTS

How do superlative superintendents look? The emotionally intelligent ones are dynamic leaders and social and relationship professionals. These superintendents *tune in* to their principals, *know* their schools, *initiate* change, *respond* to calls for assistance, and *team* successfully. The examples that follow illustrate the leadership finesse of these superlative superintendents, with a few troubling experiences thrown in regarding superintendents who are less proficient.

Tuning in to Your Principals

The job of any superintendent is challenging, and the job of the small district superintendent even more so. Small district superintendents have little or no support staff, but, just like the "big district" superintendent, are bombarded with mushrooming mandates, relentless regulations, and perpetual problems.

One of my favorite superintendents was the energetic leader of a very small, but very ambitious, school district in an enterprising rural community. This brave soul was in charge of anything and everything—K–12 support services, technology, personnel, communications, school construction, transportation, facilities, food service, and other "small" jobs like leading the classified and certificated bargaining teams and overseeing employee discipline and dismissal proceedings.

Despite my superintendent's terrifying work load, he made time for his principals. He had an open door policy. When a principal flew in with a pressing issue, he'd look up from his avalanche of paperwork and engagingly inquire, "How can I help you?" So we principals—from elementary to secondary, from newbie to warhorse—shared *everything.* We vented our frustrations, disclosed our failures, and solicited his advice. And we unabashedly bragged about our successes, counting on his enthusiastic response. By commiserating, advising, and acting as our best cheer-leader, this boss *tuned in* to our professional lives—solidifying our trust and commitment.

Know Your Schools

I once led an elementary school that shared a miniscule campus with a small secondary school and a tiny portable office that housed the super-intendent. It took just a few minutes to walk from one building to the next, but over the three years I spent at the school, not once did the superinten-dent visit my classrooms. If you find this oversight remarkable, you will find it even more so when I tell you that I worked for *three* superintendents—a different one each year.

Years later, I ended up in a small town working as a principal for a superintendent who did visit—but just twice each year. These visits came in the form of tours involving the superintendent, an entourage of district administrators, and a flock of parents and community members. Needless to say, my staff and I worked hard to put our best foot forward—and obscuring problems. We were completely stressed prior to, on edge during, and relieved after each highly orchestrated "visit."

One of the most socially sensitive superintendents I have observed in action provides a study in contrast. He visited so frequently his presence was intricately woven into the fabric of my school. This boss popped in at odd moments to chat with cooks, trade jokes with the secretaries, connect with union leaders, quiz teachers about instructional practice, and solicit impromptu goal updates from principals. And if there were problems—a gas oven venting dangerous fumes, a power outage, or an ambulance arriving for a seriously ill teacher—my superintendent was there in a heartbeat to offer support.

This highly involved superintendent exemplifies the "knowing" boss. He regularly checked the pulse of his organization by getting out of his office and into his schools, listening to and learning from his people, and supporting from the sidelines (Dolan, 1994).

Initiate Change

For superintendents, change comes hard. Just managing the day-to-day operations and myriad challenges associated with running a school district keep superintendents on the run. But achieving genuine and sustained school improvement is not easy. For superintendents picturing higher student achievement, more nurturing school climates, and safer learning environments, there are ongoing data to be analyzed, new research to be considered, and innovative programs and practices to be explored. These investigations ultimately lead to change, an unsettling and at times chaotic process that should not be undertaken by the faint of heart (Fullan, 1999).

In *Change Forces: The Sequel,* Fullan (1999) informs us "that change (planned and otherwise) unfolds in non-linear ways, that paradoxes and contradictions abound and that creative solutions arise out of interaction under conditions of uncertainty, diversity, and instability" (Fullan, p. 4). Any superintendent who has tried to engineer the adoption of a new instructional approach, a change in curriculum materials, or a shift in course content will appreciate Fullan's assessment. That's why I admire superintendents who have the drive, fortitude, and dedication necessary to undertake change as a means to improve their schools. I have worked for several successful change agents and they share two critical attributes—(1) picking substantive, relevant projects, and (2) preparing principals for a shift in direction.

I learned about the art and science of change from a deliberative superintendent who had learned about new reading practices from an internationally recognized reading specialist at a national conference. He returned to the district determined to reinvent the way reading was taught there, an amazing undertaking given that his principals were completely satisfied with the current reading program.

This boss began by educating principals—comparing reading results with more accomplished districts, bringing in powerful consultants to share the latest research on effective reading instruction, and engaging principals in enlightening discussions about reading innovations. His principals expanded their knowledge of sound reading practices and, with the superintendent's persistent nudging, coalesced around his mission. Lesson learned? This artful superintendent not only addressed the need for change, he successfully launched his new reading initiative not by imposing a new approach on his principals, but by giving them the knowledge they needed to embrace it.

Respond to Calls for Assistance

One unforgettable school day, a medically fragile preschooler in the school office collapsed in a life-threatening seizure. The school nurse attended to the convulsing child, the secretary called 911, and I summoned the Code Blue team. Code Blue? When there is a medical emergency at my school, there is a team of staff members who are called to the scene. The team's leader assists me from the sidelines as I support the school nurse, handle arriving emergency personnel, and reassure the victim's family. In this case, our Code Blue leader posted team members to direct traffic away from emergency vehicles, collected the child's medical information, and cordoned off the office so that arriving EMTs would be protected from intrusions. Superintendents are not unlike a Code Blue team leader; they respond to principals' crisis calls by providing behind the scenes support that frees principals to do their best work.

A while back I took disciplinary action against a popular staff member. This courageous move precipitated a potentially explosive reaction. Teachers and parents took sides—not mine, of course. I was inundated with requests for meetings from union reps and parents threatening to picket. To compound matters, there was a passel of complex legal issues to troubleshoot. I called my superintendent for help and his response was immediate. He acted as my "guide on the side," provided legal counsel, helped me review personnel action steps and employee safeguards with my staff, and firmly told meddling parents to "back off." Because my boss came to my rescue, the explosion I had feared was averted, and the crisis eventually resolved itself. What kind of response do principals' need from their superintendent? Immediate, substantive, and supportive!

Team Successfully

About two-thirds of the way through my career, I followed my husband to a new community and was lucky enough—or misfortunate enough as it turned out—to find a job as a principal. When I attended my first central office meeting in my new school district, the well-seasoned principal sitting next to me smiled conspiratorially then leaned in close to whisper, "Keep your mouth shut and you'll do all right." I was stunned. What on earth did she mean?

I soon learned that the superintendent's management style was the epitome of the top-down, military model that Dolan so expertly discredits in his eye-opening book, *Restructuring Our Schools* (1994). The superintendent sat at the top of the school district's organizational pyramid, supported by a platoon of district office managers who formed his cabinet. Underneath the cabinet were the elementary and secondary principals, and below them, the teachers. At the very bottom of this multilevel hierarchy were the classified staff members.

The superintendent met weekly with his cabinet; decisions made by this team, which seemed to me to be all the significant ones, were announced to the principals at monthly superintendent-principal meetings. The principals were expected to sell cabinet decisions to the troops; questioning directives was not looked on favorably. If you were lucky, your contrary opinions were condescendingly tolerated by the "higher-ups" before being completely ignored. The vocal unlucky were invited to the assistant superintendent's office for a pep talk about "teamwork."

According to my well-thumbed *Webster's*, "teamwork" is "work done by several associates with each doing a part but all subordinating personal prominence to the efficiency of the whole" (*Webster's*, 2003, p. 1282). Since the principals did not participate in the superintendent's cabinet meetings, we could not share what we were learning in the trenches, collaborate before decisions were made, and—when there were problems to address—help our leader craft an effective response. Consequently, mandates rained down from on high that the principals found to be perplexing, woefully inadequate, or just plain wrong. Many principals coped by "keeping their mouths shut."

Organizationally adept superintendents provide an antithetical example to the foregoing description of team mismanagement. They bring their principals, district assistants, and department heads together regularly to conduct business, trade information, and brainstorm solutions to problems. These superintendents expect their administrators to speak their minds. Consequently, when team members debate ways to handle a thorny issue, set districtwide goals, or develop management strategies, they coalesce around decisions that make sense. As important, there is a psychic connection that develops between the superintendent and principal that energizes and enhances professional proficiency: "Under the guidance of an EI [emotionally intelligent] leader, people feel a mutual comfort level. They share ideas from one another, make decisions collaboratively, and get things done. They form an emotional bond that helps them stay focused even amid profound change and uncertainty (Goleman et al., 2002, p. 21).

TAKE-AWAY MESSAGE

A solid relationship between a superintendent and principal underlies genuine and effective "teaming." Successful superintendents create authentic teams by tuning into their principals' needs and concerns, knowing their schools and programs, initiating change, providing ongoing support, and collaborating in a trust-building manner.

CLOSING IN ON KEY CONCEPTS

- Build trusting, enduring relationships with the members of your team.
- Tune in to the people you lead—and to their needs, concerns, problems, and successes

- Know your organization—get out of your office and into your classrooms.
- Respond to calls for help—provide immediate, substantive, and supportive assistance.
- Be fearless—initiate needed change.
- Work closely with the members of your team—be authentic!

EXTENDING YOUR THINKING

1. Do you have a sound superintendent-principal relationship? If so, how did you make this happen? If not, what changes could you make to strengthen the bond between superintendent and principal?

2. Are you a transformational leader? Why or why not? What transformational attributes do you want to acquire?

3. In what ways is your leadership style emotionally intelligent?

4. Is your administrative team authentic? In what ways? How could you strengthen the effectiveness of your team?

PART III

Leadership Team Essentials

The importance of team behavior and attitude is highlighted in Part III of our book. Chapter 5 covers this topic from the superintendent's view, underscoring the significance of communication and trust. Chapter 6 presents leadership attributes and norms from the principal's perspective. Both chapters affirm the power of healthy team relationships.

The Superintendent's Perspective

5

The Importance of Trust in Communication

The problem with communication is the illusion that it has been accomplished.

—George Bernard Shaw

Leaders often think of communication as using articles, newsletters, e-mails, television, or other vehicles to deliver their message. Their actions imply that if they just write it right, say it straight, or send it via the latest technology their audience will understand what they mean. If that were true, we would have fewer misunderstandings, and would not need to address this important topic.

MESSAGE MADNESS

The word "communication" has many meanings. For some it implies the content of the message, for others it means the use of nonverbal expression, and for still others it brings to mind the method used to communicate, such as the telephone, e-mails, or memos. This chapter illustrates that, while content, means, and methods are important concerns, none of these ensures effective communication unless it is first built on a foundation of trust. Thus, the first step in successful superintendent-principal communication is establishing trust.

The Stories

Let's look at a few examples of how a lack of trust between a superintendent and a principal led to a breakdown in communication.

"District Teacher Arrested"

This shocking headline greeted an incredulous superintendent one morning as she opened up the local newspaper. Expecting to read the latest sports headlines over coffee, she was instead caught unaware by the unsettling news that a district teacher had been arrested for child molestation. Later the superintendent learned that the principal had seen the victim alone with the teacher in the classroom after school on multiple occasions. The principal had wondered about the possibility of inappropriate behavior and considered seeking guidance from the district office. However, past experience had taught this principal that the superintendent and her personnel director typically reacted to negative information by blaming the messenger. Thus, the principal chose not to communicate this information to his supervisor.

When asked why he did not speak up, the principal said in a public statement he had kept an eye on the situation but not acted because his suspicions were likely to be unfounded. However, in private conversations the principal said that he did not trust that the information would be handled sensitively and that it might be used against him in an annual evaluation. Unfortunately, the principal kept silent because of a lack of trust in the district office and the superintendent.

"Boss's Pet Project"

The title of the e-mail immediately captured the superintendent's attention, and he quickly opened it. The e-mail, accidentally sent by a principal to the entire administrative team, left the superintendent shaken and surprised. Clearly his new district initiative had been poorly received, ridiculed, and barely understood by the principals. The superintendent was irritated and could not understand the negative response. He had communicated regularly to the principals, informed the team at several meetings about the initiative, and asked for questions and input. When he received neither objections nor questions from the administrative team, he assumed the principals were supportive.

What the superintendent did not know, unfortunately, was that principals felt he gave only lip service to participatory communication and decision making. Principals privately complained that their voices were not heard, and they were out of the decision-making loop. The clueless superintendent had no idea of the deep mistrust principals harbored about his leadership.

The superintendent had created an atmosphere of acquiescence, but not support. No one spoke up. No one openly disagreed. Fear of reprisal kept the team silent, with a pasted "Yes, sir" smile on every face. As a result, any course of action proposed and communicated by the superintendent did not receive the full support of the principals who had to implement it.

"Principals Fault the Superintendent"

This newspaper headline, which stunned the community, illustrates the powerful, negative consequences of a low-trust team. In the article, the president of the local principals' association said, on behalf of the building leaders, "What is lacking is open and safe dialogue between principals and the superintendent." He didn't stop there.

"Frankly," he continued, "we're living in a culture where everyone's afraid to make a mistake, and we've had enough. Principals are reluctant to call the superintendent if they have a question or a need. Somebody will get in trouble, when all they wanted was help fixing the problem."

Leadership team meetings are more often than not lecture sessions from the superintendent, who uses them to intimidate and control subordinates. Principals are publicly called on the carpet for perceived failures or low test scores. Private conversations belittle principals and leave them anxious and fearful. The superintendent clearly conveys who is boss through communication methods that demonstrate the power of that position.

A Lose-Lose Situation

These stories are classic examples of what happens when trust has not been built within the team. Principals who feel powerless, disrespected, unappreciated, and uninformed respond either by minimizing important communications or by not communicating at all. This behavior can lead to a number of results, all of them damaging: a delay in decision making, an underutilization of team capability, or opposition to district initiatives.

Unfortunately, all three stories came to unhappy endings. The principal who withheld his suspicions about an inappropriate student-teacher relationship was reprimanded, which led to an uneasy relationship with the superintendent, and the principal's departure from the district the following year. Contracts for both the superintendent who was viewed by the principals as a commander and the superintendent who was viewed as an intimidator were terminated by the school board within the first two years of their employment. Perhaps these are isolated examples? Alas, no. The leadership team is often a source of frustration or failure that begins with a lack of trust between the superintendent and the principals (Walton, 1998).

THE IMPORTANCE OF TRUST

The previous examples illustrate how poor communication results in destructive consequences when team trust is lacking. So how do we go about building trust that leads to productive two-way communication?

Trust and Communication

Scrap the newsletter and delete e-mails if that represents the entirety of your communication program. The preferred way to communicate is through the supervisor—the direct supervisor. When a communication issue arises between a superintendent and principals, rarely does it stem from a lack of information or an inability to use language. Rather, a communication issue indicates a lack of trust between sender and receiver. Even a great message is often not received as intended because the underlying supporting trust attributes are missing. Trust between the sender and receiver makes the difference between effective and ineffective communication. Whether or not there is trust between the superintendent and principal distinguishes strong and weak teams.

Leadership theorists maintain that trust building is one of the central mechanisms through which supervisors exert their positive influence on subordinates. A superintendent's trustworthiness affects a principal's willingness to provide that extra contribution or effort so essential to a successful school district. Moreover, a lack of trust blocks team members from working productively—not only with the superintendent, but also, frequently, with each other.

Equally important is the superintendent's behavior toward a principal's peers. A principal observes the superintendent's behavior toward the other principals and expects to receive that same kind of interaction (Lapierre, 2007). Thus, we can understand that when the superintendent's behaviors are perceived as trustworthy, principals reciprocate.

Lack of Trust Indicators

Trust is complex. Team members hold a variety of perspectives on a single situation. These differences result over time as individuals develop unique "mental models" or "mindsets" (Walton, 1998) about what observed behaviors indicate. Alert, effective leaders recognize the potential of a variety of interpretations or misinterpretations of an action or behavior. They are alert to indicators of trust-reducing behaviors and take action steps to build trust (Therkelsen & Fiebich, 2003). Superintendents should watch for the following problems among team members and "red flag" areas that the team can address through trust-building activities:

- Acts more concerned with his or her own welfare than anything else
- Sends mixed messages so others never know where they stand in a situation
- Avoids taking responsibility for actions
- Jumps to conclusions without checking the facts first
- Makes excuses or blames others when things do not work out
- Interprets whatever is said as though the speaker has a hidden agenda
- Keeps information "close to the chest"
- Does not reveal thinking, and lacks transparency
- Uses information to manipulate outcomes
- Undermines decisions unfavorable to his or her cause
- Works his or her own agenda and makes backroom deals

Presence of Trust Indicators

A trusting team collaborates, aligns activity for a more effective outcome, and extends the leadership of the superintendent into the schools. Use the following checklist to assess the presence of trust in your team. Provide recognition for taking steps in the right direction. In a high-trust environment, team members can do the following:

- Express thoughts, opinions, and feelings without fear
- Cooperate and not engage in right-wrong, win-lose competitions
- Feel listened to and valued for what they say, even though others may not agree
- Communicate honestly without distorting information
- Show confidence in team members' abilities
- Keep promises and commitments
- Look for ways to help each other

PORTRAITS OF TRUST

Trust is so important to the team, yet so easily misunderstood. Thus illustrations of the basic attributes will paint a picture of trust in practice. The belief that a superintendent will be benevolent, caring, competent, open, and reliable corresponds to the extent to which a principal is willing to risk becoming vulnerable and trusting in the relationship. The stories below describe these five trust characteristics and the effects on principals.

Benevolence and Caring

The principals in the Happy Valley School District still talk about John, a sensitive and caring man who was the superintendent ten years ago. Stories of his genuine nurturing abound. Ann still gets teary eyed remembering when her father passed away. John called and came over, substituted for her in meetings, and went to the school board to fight for extra days for Ann so she could help her widowed mother with family matters.

Benevolence and caring are most frequently identified in the research as the priority attributes of trust. Both benevolence and caring inspire a belief that one will be protected and not harmed by the other. This belief may stem from observing such behavior in the other person, past mutual experiences, or the reputation of that person as reported by colleagues (Fromme, 2005).

Benevolent leaders desire to "do good" aside from any personal motive or personal gain. Benevolent leaders show consideration and sensitivity for the principal's personal needs and interests. They act in a way that protects a principal's personal interests, and they refrain from exploiting principals for the benefit of their own interests. Thus the superintendent who "goes to bat" to obtain salary increases for principals is likely to be perceived as benevolent. Conversely, the superintendent who obtains a salary increase for principals simply to make an argument for a similar personal increase is not acting with benevolence. A caring, benevolent leader is genuinely interested in the well-being of others. Showing consideration and sensitivity for others' needs and interests, both personal or professional, is the first hallmark of trust.

Competence

Competence is the next most frequently mentioned attribute found in the various definitions of trust (Fromme, 2005), although many people mistake intellectual prowess as the sole indicator of competence. Consider Karen, a superintendent who takes the "super" part of her title seriously. She attends seminars with world-class leaders, reads all the latest journals page by page, and continually sends out "must read" material to the principals. Her intellectual prowess and grasp of subject matter in a variety of areas are evident. However, intellectual activity is not the sole evidence of competence.

Like Karen, many superintendents define competence as demonstrating superior intelligence and adequate technical skills for the job. However, to be truly competent, one must also acquire skills in a wide range of human relations such as conflict resolution, active listening, and problem solving.

This human relations component of competence was further supported in a recent survey on evaluation standards in Washington State (Derrington, 2007). Principals were asked what skills and attributes they believe are necessary for a superintendent to be an effective supervisor and evaluator of the principals' performance. The highest-ranking and most frequently mentioned attribute was interpersonal relations. The lowest-ranking attribute was professional intelligence, including being well-read and knowledgeable (Derrington).

Openness

Open internal communication is vital in keeping morale high and employees happy, thus helping to ensure an effective work environment. Satisfaction with one's job and with management is influenced by a subordinate's perception of a supervisor's openness.

Superintendent Marie keeps no secrets from the principals. She is transparent with both feelings and facts. She shares information freely without going overboard. She invites the team to actively participate in solving problems and developing solutions. Principals fully understand the issues, sense that they are an integral part of important events in the district, and accurately convey the information to school staff.

Sharing power through involving and informing is good practice. Communication and shared decision making are hallmarks of openness. To allow oneself to be vulnerable to sharing decision making and power is critical in a trusting relationship (Fromme, 2005).

Reliability

Frank, a dedicated superintendent, makes time for principals according to their schedules, which is usually before and after school. He is consistently available, returning calls promptly and responding to requests diligently. In times of crisis or adversity he remains even-tempered and calm. His behavior is predictable.

Trust is cultivated when our behavior is consistent with the expectations others have of us. Behavior that earns trust can come from the simple act of returning phone calls promptly, when such an act is the norm. Trust is reduced, though, when our actions are erratic and unpredictable. When subordinates are unsure what a superior's response will be, even in the most ordinary of circumstances, trust cannot find a foothold and communication suffers.

Trust Building Takes Time

Developing trust is an interactive process that builds over time. As positive experiences accumulate, people become more willing to extend greater trust (Walton, 1998). The degree to which people know and trust each other affects the degree to which people can agree. When mutual credibility exists between people, decisions are reached more readily. There is less need to check and test premises and assumptions because each person involved is believable. Subordinates who trust their supervisors are willing to accept a degree of vulnerability in that relationship, because they feel confident about the supervisor's behavior.

Interpersonal trust opens the doors of risk and vulnerability because of one person's dependence on another. Yet it is a door that must be opened to achieve and sustain trust and subsequently develop effective communication with the leadership team. I have consistently observed that a high-trust environment promotes genuine communication, which in turn results in aligned team actions.

Trust admittedly is difficult to achieve and time consuming to develop. Unfortunately, problems often occur early in the team formation and relationship-building process. Consider the newspaper examples at the beginning of the chapter: Every situation occurred in the first two years of the superintendents' tenure.

"So," a superintendent colleague pointedly asked me, "how do you build trust quickly?" It can be done, because most people will, at first, give trust freely. They go into the relationship expecting it to be one of mutual respect. That's the good news. The bad news is that this gift is provisional. Thus the first year of interaction is critical. A team unfamiliar with a newcomer suspends judgment for a time. Being new in a position is like standing in fresh cement. You have an opportunity to make an impression, but others' opinions harden quickly and are very difficult to change.

Developing Strategies

Superintendents and principals agree on the importance of trust in a team relationship (Derrington, 2007). This practitioner knowledge is supported by accepted researched knowledge (Fromme, 2005). However, to be truly effective, the attributes of trust must be translated into meaningful team behaviors. It is behavior that influences us. We can observe behavior, address behavior, and hold others accountable for their behavior. The effective leadership team works to create positive behaviors that develop trust. The following section illustrates that even use of e-mail can provide occasions to build trust.

E-mail Communications and Relationships

Mention e-mail to busy superintendents and principals and a sigh of frustration circles the group like the "wave" at a baseball game. According to an article by Michelle Kessler in *USA Today*, October 5, 2007, "White-collar workers often receive 140 messages a day." My discussions with superintendents and principals indicate that this number is fairly accurate and may surprisingly be lower than averages in some districts.

But while e-mail is often considered a nuisance by busy administrators, it can have a positive aspect. Albert Huang, a professor in the Management Information Systems Department, University of the Pacific, California, conducted a study on e-mail communication between professionals and their immediate supervisor (Huang, 2002). He found that frequency of e-mail is a significant factor in building interpersonal relationships. Although the data did not explain why that is so, Huang hypothesizes that frequent e-mail communication leads to more exchanges of information, making it easy for the team to stay in contact and providing opportunities for relationships to grow, especially if more social information is also exchanged (Huang). However, frequency of e-mail communication by itself is not sufficient to develop trust, as the following section explains.

Trust Tips for E-mail Use

E-mail is text based, and thus is incapable of transmitting nontextual cues, such as body language, tone of voice, or facial expressions. So choose e-mail as the communication medium with information you do not need to communicate face to face. For example, e-mail is appropriate to make general announcements, such as a notice of a scheduled meeting, but can be treacherous and potentially disastrous when it is used to convey information about a delicate situation or one laden with conflict, for example. E-mail can have an impact on the quality of the communication exchanges by creating a higher level of mutual trust if handled with care. Use the following suggestions for effective use of e-mail.

- Wait and reread e-mails before sending if emotions are involved.
- Address an angry e-mail to yourself first and be sure you want to send it before doing so.
- Think through the message and compose a thorough communication.
- Avoid sending multiple follow-ups with every additional thought you have. Countless e-mails make you seem disorganized.
- Always acknowledge the positive before unleashing the negative. A balanced perspective is necessary.

- Selectively cc (carbon copy). Interoffice "wars" have been started over a cc that indicated the sender was openly engaging in a "CYA" (cover your a**) move, a definite indicator of a lack of trust.

Meetings as Trust-Building Time

Meetings provide occasions to do our work in public in front of our peers. Think carefully about the management of these group sessions. The tone you set can build up or break down trust. As the person with formal authority, the superintendent will be watched closely by the other group members. Because subordinates will take their behavioral cues from the leader, superintendents need to model desired behavior at every opportunity. How well the behaviors are performed is not as critical as the sincere attempt to practice the interpersonal behavior that demonstrates trust.

Leaders of organizations will benefit from watching a good staff developer. These professionals know how to lighten things up and relieve tensions when the agenda is tough, or when interpersonal conflicts surface. They use all sorts of simple strategies: ice breakers, appropriate humor, relaxation techniques, refreshments, raffles, and motivational music or video clips, to name just a few. They are masters at watching the body language cues of the team members, then adjusting the agenda accordingly.

These techniques and others can be found in a variety of resources. Two of my favorite books on the subject are *Mining for Group Gold* by Thomas A. Kayser (1990) and *Still More Games Trainers Play* by Edward Scannell and John Newstrom (1991).

Assessing the Team's Interactions

Evaluate your team communication behaviors following the meeting. Group data can be collected and shared using the tools learned in the school improvement process and found in books like *Data Analysis for Continuous School Improvement* by Victoria L. Bernhardt, PhD (2004). I adopted these ideas and developed a simple survey listing the desired behaviors of my leadership team, then applied a Likert scale indicating degree of agreement or disagreement with demonstrated behaviors in each meeting to average the group's anonymous responses. The results, when shared with the group using visual depictions such as graphs and charts, indicate group opinion of its own behavior. Feedback can be examined over time and steps taken to change strategies and celebrate progress.

The superintendent plays a key role in developing trust by using team data and feedback. The superintendent, by accepting open and honest feedback from the survey results, models willingness to change, a nondefensiveness to constructive criticism, and an openness to the team's opinion. The team becomes self-corrective and engaged in continuous improvement through data-based feedback (Rivero, 1998). Take your group's emotional pulse through brief but informative surveys designed to improve your team communication.

TAKE-AWAY MESSAGE

Interpersonal trust is the glue of day-to-day life in a leadership team. A superintendent and the principals must understand and trust each other at the most fundamental level because the work is significant, profound, and complex. This trust is gained over time and in the context of ongoing interactions with peers. Moreover, the team must agree on definable, measurable behaviors to establish a trusting relationship. This consensus creates an environment of trust conducive to honest and ongoing communication about what is working and what is not. This is the first step to creating a resonant team (Goleman, 1997). Insight leads to impact.

CLOSING IN ON KEY CONCEPTS

- Trust is the foundation of effective communication.
- High-trust teams risk, care, and share.
- Teams that trust each other collaborate and thus are able to achieve districtwide objectives.
- Defined team trust behaviors can be assessed.
- Norms and meeting behaviors should be evaluated regularly to increase team performance.
- E-mail as a form of communication can build trust when used appropriately.
- Professional behavior should always be modeled by the supervisor!

EXTENDING YOUR THINKING

1. What characteristics of your leadership team and superintendent-principal interactions demonstrate that a trusting relationship exists?

2. What steps can you take toward improved communications?

3. What are you personally willing to do to promote trust within your administrative team?

The Principal's Perspective   **6**

*Communication Expectations
and Relationships*

---

*Very little in our lives is more important and more persuasive than
our relationships with those we care about and with whom we work.
And very little is more inscrutable and problematic. Relationships
can be as taxing and toxic as they can be replenishing and fulfilling.*

      —Roland S. Barth (2003, p. xi)

Teddy Roosevelt once admonished, "Do what you can, with what you have, where you are" (Peter, 1977, p. 37). I have long wondered if the old soldier had had his Rough Riders in mind when he said that—leading people is tough business. Whether you lead people on the battlefield or in the workplace—which at times feels like a battlefield—you must get people to work as a team. For principals and superintendents, this endeavor becomes a relationship nightmare when the ethics and collaborative skills of team members are weak or out of sync, or both.

CRITICAL ATTRIBUTES

What do I mean by *ethics* and *collaboration?* An Internet search yielded more than 200 million citations and volumes of discussion regarding these esoteric concepts, but these straightforward dictionary definitions will do for our purposes: Ethics: "The discipline dealing with what is good and bad" (*Webster's*, 2003, p. 429) and Collaborate: "To work jointly with others or together" (p. 243). Sounds simple: work together and behave.

These expectations are apparently mystifying, though, given the sad state of supervisor-subordinate relationships in the workplace, school districts included.

PRINCIPALS' PERSPECTIVE

Nothing is more important to the career success of principals than their relationship with their superintendent. I surveyed principals about this vital variable to learn more about it, and gleaned some revealing stories.

Superintendent Attributes

The four principals whose comments are highlighted below are *2006 National Distinguished Principal Award* winners. Their impressive record of school leadership totals more than eighty-five years between them. Although their professional experiences varied, each identified well-developed interpersonal skills and unquestionable personal and professional ethics as being critical for a boss.

Principal DellaBarca

Louis DellaBarca has successfully led schools in New Jersey for thirty-one years and has had the pleasure of working for superintendents who not only understood Louis's job, but who also gave him unfailing support. These sterling superintendents solicited Louis's views, recognized his accomplishments, and treated him with the utmost respect. Louis has also worked for superintendents who were startlingly insensitive. Louis laments, "They didn't listen, were openly mean, and were demeaning to others." When it comes to leadership style, Louis believes that sensitivity on the part of a superintendent is essential. Or, as he politely suggests, "A little kindness and understanding would be appreciated!"

Principal Rafferty

Another strong voice for people skills is Charlotte Rafferty, an exemplary principal in Florida for nearly two decades. Charlotte has been fortunate to work for superintendents who earned her trust and confidence. These were the ones who listened to her, asked about her challenges, and applauded her successes. Unfortunately, Charlotte also has endured superintendents who were clueless about how to work with subordinates. Charlotte says, "They did not understand human nature—they wanted all the credit, never gave principals any recognition, and never asked if they could help in a hard situation." Charlotte wants a superintendent who "likes principals and believes in them and their work." And, as an added bonus, Charlotte appreciates a boss who can pass this litmus test—return her phone calls!

Principal Dillon

Angela Dillon hails from Georgia and brings twenty-five years of solid experience to her position. She talks enthusiastically about one of her favorite superintendents: "He has high ethical standards, is very committed, and works tirelessly to improve our school system for our students." Admirable! But Angela has also suffered from superintendents whom she describes as uncommitted and untrustworthy. "The status quo was accepted," Angela says, "and ethics were a real challenge!" Angela appreciates superintendents who articulate a strong sense of purpose and whose productivity is more than sufficient to carry out their vision. As important, Angela values a boss in whom she can place her trust.

Principal Drake

Billie Jo Drake is a top-notch principal from Kansas with ten years in the trenches. She has had good luck with superintendents, whom she joyfully describes as "wonderful!" What would be a problem for Principal Drake? "Having a boss," she reports, "who had a difficult time making decisions for which blame could be placed on him or who prefaced everything with some other administrator's name first." Billie Jo asserts, "Superintendents must be willing to make decisions and have a 'the buck stops here' attitude."

Principals' Expectations

What kind of boss do our four principals want? Superintendents who work well, work hard, and work right. These superintendents have a strong ethical sense, demonstrate first-rate collaborative skills, and bring a heartfelt sensitivity to their engagement with people. Aren't these the same expectations superintendents have for principals?

SUPERINTENDENTS' PERSPECTIVE

To get the superintendents' perspective, I went to trusted sources—four highly successful superintendents recognized for their leadership accomplishments: Walt Bigby, Doug Nelson, John Pope, and Gene Sharratt.

LEADERSHIP ATTRIBUTES

a. Gaining the trust and cooperation of staff members and clients

b. Staying current with educational theory, curriculum content, and best practices

c. Growing professionally

d. Putting the achievement and welfare of students first

e. Articulating a strong sense of purpose

f. Working collaboratively with others to set and reach goals

g. Leading staff effectively through organization and program changes

h. Demonstrating unquestionable personal and professional ethics

i. Conveying an optimistic outlook

j. Being an "instructional leader" by teaching, sharing, and leading school improvement work

k. Managing finances and other resources competently

l. Putting people and program needs ahead of one's own

m. Demonstrating efficiency, strong management skills, and high productivity

n. Supervising and evaluating subordinates fairly, sensitively, and accurately

o. Observing pertinent policies, procedures, and legal parameters

p. Developing leadership qualities in others

q. Using assessment results to set goals, develop plans, and evaluate progress

r. Seeking input from others before making decisions

s. Gaining the confidence of community members

t. Handling problems, conflicts, and crises skillfully

u. Offering support and assistance to teachers and administrators

v. Staying visible

Together, they have eighty years of administrative experience at the district level—fifty-eight as superintendents, eighteen as assistants, and four as curriculum leaders. I sent each a list of twenty-three school leadership qualities covering instructional leadership, school management, and interpersonal skills, with instructions to choose the ten characteristics they most valued in a principal.

Principal Attributes

Three of the above attributes were identified by all four superintendents: (a) gaining the trust and cooperation of staff members and clients, (d) putting the achievement and welfare of students first, and (f) working collaboratively with others to set and reach goals. That makes sense. These relationship-building skills will earn the confidence of students, staff, and clients—and of the superintendent. Four other qualities were selected by at least three of the four superintendents; of these, one concerned the active use of assessment results. Three attributes, however, had to do with character traits and interpersonal skills: (h) demonstrating unquestionable personal and professional ethics, (j) being an "instructional leader" by teaching, sharing, and leading school improvement work, and (t) handling problems, conflicts, and crises skillfully. Like the distinguished principals presented earlier, these four superintendents affirmed that integrity and the ability to work well with others are all important.

When I quizzed these superintendents about principal behavior, they had a lot to share.

Superintendent Nelson

Doug Nelson, whose work is highlighted in Chapter 8 of this book, has more than thirty years of administrative experience. He has led school districts ranging in size from twenty-two hundred to nearly sixteen thousand students. He earned a doctorate degree in educational leadership and merited Washington State's prestigious *Christa McAuliffe Outstanding Superintendent Award.* Doug has supervised "blue ribbon" principals, but has also worked with school leaders who were troublesome. Doug believes that principal success requires what he calls "people orientation." This includes the ability to forge productive relationships, bring a positive outlook to collaborative endeavors, and communicate with a high degree of finesse. Doug's core beliefs about superintendent-principal relationships are captured in the Q & A that follows.

SUPERINTENDENT NELSON Q & A

Cathie: What kind of relationship do you want with principals?

Doug: A relationship built on trust is the optimal situation. I try to hire the very best people for each job and try not to "settle." When you hire well, then trust becomes natural.

Cathie: How about communication—what's important to you?

Doug: I want principals to keep me informed. I stress "no surprises," so if they know I will get a call from a mad parent, they should have briefed me prior to getting that call. In doing so, they demonstrate the courage to lead.

Cathie: What else do you expect?

Doug: We are a people business and I expect that principals treat staff members, patrons, parents, and students with dignity and respect. I do not expect to have to remind them of this expectation too often.

Cathie: You've worked with some "problem principals." What type is the worst?

Doug: The worst do not have a sense of leading a group of professionals. It is a misperception of the role of a leader—it's not about power, but collegiality.

Cathie: When it comes to principal effectiveness—what do you look for?

Doug: I look for openness, the courage to lead, and the ability to face "brutal facts" with optimism. And strong relationships with all stakeholders, including the superintendent!

Superintendent Sharratt

Dr. Gene Sharratt directs the Superintendent Certification Program for Washington State University, and has played a leadership role at the district, regional, and state levels for more than twenty-five years. He has extensive administrative experience—as principal, assistant superintendent, and superintendent. He has taught graduate-level curriculum and educational leadership classes throughout his career, and has provided consultation to schools and districts in his role as School Improvement Specialist for Washington State's Office of the Superintendent of Public Instruction. Gene has published countless articles about learning and leadership, and holds numerous awards, including Washington State School Superintendent of the Year and the National Educational Administrator of the Year Award.

Gene's perfect principal demonstrates "core values—ethical behavior, integrity, compassion, and service to others." This is followed by "a total commitment to children, learning for all, and strong relationship building skills." Gene believes that principals should have a "strong sense of purpose and the ability to communicate the school's mission to all stakeholders." He also emphasizes the importance of "organization and management." He wisely observes that principals "must be able to manage well to lead well. It is not an either-or, but rather a strong blend of both that contributes to a highly effective school."

The weak principals Gene has encountered could not "read the context of the school." He explains: "Principals who are not intuitive, not aware of the culture and climate of the school, have a challenging time assessing the need for change and how to lead and develop people."

Superintendent Pope

John Pope is currently a vice president with a major financial management firm. At one time, though, he was the successful superintendent of a five thousand–student school district in a small coastal community. During his tenure, John was recognized as an outstanding superintendent. His award for his achievement was not the usual wall plaque, however, but rather a ticket to a three-week leadership symposium at Columbia University—a perfect prize, given his reflective nature.

John appreciated principals who were open to new ideas and "willing to stretch." In particular, he valued the "smart" ones who stayed focused on their goals, who were strong communicators, and who were savvy enough to solve their own problems. These were the ones who best helped John carry out his mission to improve schools. John shares additional insights about leadership and relationships in the following Q & A.

SUPERINTENDENT POPE Q & A

Cathie: When you became a superintendent, what was your mission?

John: I felt that my interest in school improvement could be pursued at the senior level effectively. This turned out to be quite a challenge. In fact, those most capable of making change happen—or stopping it all together—are the teachers!

Cathie: Change is tough for many teachers. How do superintendents handle "hold outs"?

John: Someone who "believes" [in the change] has to take the reins and provide leadership, gentle motivation, support, and a myriad of other things to facilitate change.

Cathie: How do principals fit in to this picture?

John: The partnership between the superintendent and the principal is essential. A quality principal will facilitate the relationship between the teachers and the superintendent as well as between their public and the district.

Cathie: So relationship skills are vital.

John: It is important to follow policies and to manage well, but without strong communication and collaborative skills principals will fail.

Cathie: What underlies a successful superintendent-principal relationship?

John: For a superintendent and a principal to function effectively—and not at cross purposes—it is essential to have an open and honest relationship. This requires the superintendent to earn the trust of the principal. Dishonesty and secrecy from either party will ultimately damage the relationship. Both administrators must take a leap of faith—to trust. This ensures attainment of what they intend to accomplish in the best interest of kids.

Cathie: What if trust is missing?

John: The superintendent must take responsibility and work with the principal to build mutual trust. The goal is to earn trust through mutual respect and open communication.

Cathie: What has been your biggest disappointment?

John: Principals who blame parents, teachers, other principals, and the superintendent for anything not going their way!

Superintendent Bigby

Walt Bigby has served at the school district leadership level for twenty-four years—twenty of them as superintendent—before taking the reins of a four-county education service district serving fifty-two thousand students from fifteen school districts. Walt earned a doctorate in education administration and twice received the Washington Association of School Administrators' Award of Merit. He also snapped up a State Recognition Award from the Association for Supervision and Curriculum Development (ASCD). Walt's team-building leadership style is captured in Chapter 2 of this book. His expectations for principals and superintendents are crystal clear: "They should see themselves as part of a team committed to the success of children. This means developing a school's identity within a districtwide framework, or common set of beliefs, believing that the improvement of schools is based upon data and research, and demonstrating that this work is continuous."

Walt looks for principals who have integrity and strong instructional leadership skills. He is impatient with principals who are "selfish and non-collaborative" and who "put adults before students." I asked Walt when he knew things were going well between a superintendent and a principal and his response reflected his beliefs about the focus of educational endeavors: "Things are going well when both the superintendent and the principal see themselves as part of a team, committed to the success of students."

Superintendent Expectations

The profiled superintendents have substantial expectations for principals and share the desire for sound relationships with their school leaders. Trusting relationships build on ethical behavior, effective collaboration, and open communication. The foregoing discussion about leadership behaviors and relationships, however, leaves unanswered questions: How do superintendents communicate their expectations to principals? And, conversely, how do principals communicate their needs to their superintendent?

EXPECTATION DEVELOPMENT

Administrative job descriptions are in place in most school districts, but few spell out the ethical and collaborative behaviors needed for team success. Superintendents and principals need more than a list of job responsibilities: they need directives that spell out what professional conduct and healthy working relationships look like. Barth (2003) insightfully called standards for professional conduct working rules: "Working rules are the norms of personal and professional behavior required for individuals in the workplace to stay on friendly terms and, in addition, to produce a distinguished product" (p. xxi). I use a Code of Ethics and Collaboration (CEC) for workplace expectations, a plan I develop soon after taking over a school. I learned long ago that successful school relationships are founded on clearly communicated expectations (McEwan, 2005).

My first CEC for school administrators was prepared when my exceptional superintendent began talking retirement. Is anything more unnerving than to learn that the boss you are in sync with is about to depart? My superintendent was a joy to work with and had crafted a well-functioning administrative team. Would a new superintendent do as well? Could there be a shift in expectations? Would the effortless way our team worked together falter? It was time to document what was going well and how we made it work.

When I proposed a CEC for our administrative team, the superintendent and principals readily agreed. The code would provide continuity when a new superintendent—or principal for that matter—joined our team. Creating a code would also give us the chance to communicate the expectations we had for each other and serve as a standard against which we evaluated the efficacy of our professionalism. As it turned out, there was an unexpected gift: as we dug deeply into the meaning of ethics and collaboration, we dug deeply into ourselves.

Creating the Code

I used a multistep process to create the code. This work began with a review of my school's CEC (McEwan, 2005) and our administrative evaluation instrument (Granite Falls School District, 2005). This glimpse yielded an outline for the code and a partial list of expectations.

Additional norms sprang from my own administrative experiences. I called to mind the superintendent whose upbeat outlook lifted my spirits, the pessimistic business manager who never failed to cast a dispiriting pall over every endeavor, the uncommunicative curriculum director who left me ill prepared to advance new initiatives, and the visionary principal whose engaging collaborative skills provided a powerful model for me and every other administrator. And then there were the superintendents who failed to support their principals and the principals who by word, action, or intentional inaction undermined their superintendents. Ironically, coming up with working rules was a breeze.

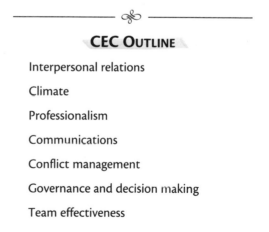

CEC OUTLINE

Interpersonal relations

Climate

Professionalism

Communications

Conflict management

Governance and decision making

Team effectiveness

Next I tapped into the workplace experiences of my colleagues by engaging them in an activity whimsically titled "Team Members From Hell" (Resource A). Each team member—superintendent, principals, business manager, and department heads—responded to this prompt:

> Think back on your career and to the many relationships you have had with superintendents, personnel directors, business managers, program directors, elementary and secondary principals, and administrative support staff. Are there supervisors and colleagues who are forever etched in your memory because they caused you untold grief, made you furious, provoked sleepless nights, or drove you nuts? What was it about these irksome individuals that set them apart? For the next eight minutes, write about these team members from hell. Who were they? How did they conduct business? What did they say or not say, do or not do? (Resource A)

Participant engagement was instantaneous and intense; the opportunity to tell "stories out of school" about dysfunctional colleagues had struck a chord.

When it came time to share their frustrating tales, no one held back. The principals complained about superintendents who had favorites, colleagues who violated confidentiality, and department heads who wasted principals' time by running directionless meetings. The district-level administrators described principals who impeded their work by being late with reports, overspending allocations, ignoring district policies, or failing to follow grant parameters. And our superintendent lamented administrators at all levels who stymied district initiatives through inaction or just plain incompetence.

The "Team Members From Hell" exercise yielded an abundance of ideas for workplace expectations. As I fleshed out the second draft of the CEC I kept in mind that these norms were for my team—and not just for me—and that the code needed every administrator's approval before completion. At a follow-up meeting, team members were given the chance to assess the value of each code expectation and make suggestions (Resource B). This led to a few changes, such as dropping a team-building expectation about socializing outside of work hours because it was not deemed essential. In addition, language was added concerning prompt responses to e-mails and voice mails at the urging of district administrators who had a tough time getting information from busy principals.

When we looked at the final draft of our CEC at a subsequent meeting, we personalized code expectations by asking ourselves two questions: "Are these the professional behaviors we aspire to?" and "Is this how we want to conduct business?" A deep discussion about the meaning of professionalism and team collaboration followed. In the process, we learned a lot about each other—our fears, hopes, disappointments, and ideals. When the superintendent called for approval of the CEC, it was unanimous.

✂

ADMINISTRATIVE TEAM CEC

We will build a high-quality administrative team and maintain supportive relationships by observing the following expectations:

Interpersonal Relations

- Recognize that each administrator brings education, experiences, and talents that are unique and valuable.
- Demonstrate that every job is important and everyone deserves respect.
- Show loyalty by representing team members positively within the district and community.

Climate

- Communicate openly, do our part when help is needed, and maintain an optimistic outlook.
- Look for humor and laugh a lot.

Professionalism

- Demonstrate integrity by being responsible, trustworthy, honest, and fair.
- Observe district policies and procedures, state and federal regulations, and school and department budget parameters.
- Become better administrators through self-evaluation, goal setting, and collaboration.
- Stay current with educational research and best practices through inservice, school visitations, innovative projects, and professional reading.
- Support colleagues by serving as mentors, providing consultation, and sharing successful practices.

Communications

- Communicate knowledge, ideas, and opinions in a constructive manner.
- Keep team members involved in and informed about school- and district-level decisions and activities.
- Be professional in verbal and written communications.
- Respect confidentiality as it pertains to students and their families, teachers and support staff, the administrative team, and the school board.

(Continued)

(Continued)

Conflict Management

- Use face-to-face communication when major concerns arise.
- Employ conflict-resolution strategies (e.g., "I" messages, agreeing to disagree, facilitators) to resolve disagreements.
- Model forgiveness by letting go of past hurts or disappointments.

Governance and Decision Making

- Acknowledge that the administrative team works for the school board by supporting the board's mission and decisions.
- Recognize that school- and district-level administrators work for the superintendent by supporting the superintendent's mission and directives.
- Consult with principals and district administrators before decisions that affect them are made.
- Use nondivisive decision-making strategies (e.g., decision by consensus, surveys, troubleshooting committees).

Team Effectiveness

- Contribute to the effectiveness of meetings by arriving on time, being prepared, listening attentively, avoiding side conversations, and sharing information in a time-conscious manner.
- Share school and district resources (e.g., basic education funds, grant allocations, staffing) as equitably as possible, given district, school, and program needs.
- Submit required records, reports, and communiqués to the appropriate team members in a timely fashion.
- Show consideration for team members by responding to e-mail, voice mail, and service requests promptly.

Revisiting Expectations

Our CEC was completed mid-year but not forgotten; six months later, at an administrative retreat, we revisited the code. We engaged in an interactive exercise (Resource C) that called on trios of administrators to design and perform skits depicting code violations. The job for observers was to identify which CEC expectation was being trampled on. The "actors" were enthusiastic and the skits cleverly constructed. One team, for example, depicted our superintendent announcing a new directive to our administrative team, then showed a follow-up phone call between two principals who trashed our boss for adding more work to their plates. These disloyal subordinates even agreed to covertly ignore the new directive—a violation of the CEC norm "supporting the superintendent's mission and directives." This bold team of performers was promptly fired by our actual superintendent, provoking considerable laughter. The skits provided a novel and at times amusing way to review working rules.

Code Violators

We have a strong administrative team but what if we didn't? What if one or more members were code violators? I learned early on in my career as principal to use my school's CEC to set expectations for errant staff members. In most instances an individual conference was all it took. If need be, though, I would use the code to support disciplinary action: "When I had to non-renew a probationary teacher for professional misconduct, the code of ethics became a valuable tool at a meeting with the union reps. One look at the code and it was clear that the teacher knew better than to engage in the behavior that she did" (Cathie West, as quoted in McEwan, 2005, pp. 9–10).

A superintendent might use an administrative CEC similarly with principals and district administrators whose interpersonal skills or level of professionalism fails to meet the mark. But what if it's the superintendent who is the code violator? As a principal, I rely on face-to-face communication to convey concerns to my boss. If the superintendent listens and takes corrective action, I have done my boss a favor. If not, the bottom line is that I am hired to work for and support my superintendent. This leads us back to Teddy Roosevelt's charge: "Do what you can, with what you have, where you are." Principals may find themselves working for superintendents whose finesse with people is weak or whose interpretation of professionalism is shaky. My advice to principals is to "do what you can" to get the best from your boss. Stay positive and be constructive. Communicate and give good council—and always model professional behavior. In other words, follow your administrative CEC.

TAKE-AWAY MESSAGE

Superior superintendent-principal teams do not happen by accident; they are carefully crafted. Crystal-clear expectations and open communication are prerequisites, as is the commitment to ethical, collaborative, and professional behavior.

CLOSING IN ON KEY CONCEPTS

- Strong interpersonal skills and unquestionable professional ethics are essential leadership attributes.

- Quality collaborative skills are requisite for healthy workplace relationships.
- Trusting relationships spring from ethical behavior, collaboration, and communication.
- Standards for professional conduct—such as a CEC—tell team members what is expected and how to behave.
- Superintendents support principals by understanding the complexity of their job, soliciting their views, leading collaboratively, recognizing accomplishments, and offering assistance.
- Principals support their superintendent by supporting initiatives and directives, maintaining high standards, communicating openly and constructively, collaborating effectively, and staying positive.
- Professionals always model professional behavior.

EXTENDING YOUR THINKING

1. Team discussions about goals, policy, and practice never come easily. Discussions can become uncomfortable or even contentious. What have you done to keep team communication constructive?

2. Trusting relationships spring from ethical behavior, collaboration, and communication. What does ethical behavior and collaboration look like in your district?

3. How do you communicate your expectations? What do you do about team members who openly violate the norms you have set?

PART IV

Leadership Learning

In Part IV, the last section of our book, we focus on the value of individual and team growth. Chapter 7 presents strategies superintendents can use to strengthen team capacity, and Chapter 8 reveals ways superintendents perfect principal performance, and how this effort contributes to the superintendents' own growth. Both presentations stress the importance of ongoing "leadership learning."

The Superintendent's Perspective

7

Cultivating Team Capacity

Teams, not individuals, are the fundamental learning unit in modern organizations.

—Peter Senge (1993, p. 10)

The learning organization concept was introduced by Peter Senge (1993) in his book *The Fifth Discipline: The Art and Practice of the Learning Organization.* Senge's work describing how organizations learn is the foundation for team learning and professional development communities in schools. His ideas appeal naturally to educators because they understand learning concepts and how to apply these concepts to school teams.

THE LEARNING TEAM

We define *learning teams* as groups of professionals who—both together and through a collaborative process—increase results, knowledge, and competence within the group by contributing their individual experiences, insights, and skills to the group. The examples in the following pages illustrate that the effective superintendent-principal team learns from its collective successes and failures. They share knowledge and experience, which in turn inspires their continued professional growth. Most important, they embed this learning in their daily work at the school.

Improve Your Collective Competence

Principals are busy enough just running the school and keeping teachers focused on learning. Superintendents likewise can fill a day with school board and community obligations. Moreover, the annual evaluation of these leaders typically rates performance on these responsibilities. So why should teams shift from familiar and perhaps comfortable team interactions to one that may challenge the status quo? Why should successful principals expand their focus from leadership at the school to include a role as learners with their peers? Why will successful superintendents relinquish control to become vulnerable as a peer learner with the team? The answer to these questions is that leaders with this learning orientation expand and deepen their skills and become more competent and confident on the job when results demonstrate success. Through building team collegiality and sharing ideas they acquire a new set of tools for school improvement.

Contrast an orientation on the accomplishment of learning (a learning orientation) with an orientation on the mere appearance of that accomplishment (a performance orientation). A performance orientation ensures that teams will work hard to look good. Conversely, a learning orientation ensures that teams will work smart to actually perform better (Garvin, 2000).

Reviewing the Learning Community

The literature is clear: creating professional learning communities is one of the best ways for school staff to collaborate and focus on learning. These learning communities provide time to reflect, deepen understanding, and create dialogue and engagement on a variety of school issues. The term "professional learning community" (PLC) has been coined to describe a group of professionals that come together to learn in a supportive, self-created community. Using the National Staff Development Council standards and applying these concepts to the leadership team, an effective PLC

- meets regularly,
- focuses on learning, both that of the students and that of the team members,
- solves problems,
- commits to continuous improvement and experimentation, and
- engages members in improving their daily work.

Principals and superintendent typically implement learning communities at the schools and focus on teacher development. I propose that the learning team concept also can be used with the leadership team to increase collaborative learning.

APPLYING THE PROFESSIONAL LEARNING COMMUNITY CONCEPTS

Principals and the superintendent need time to come together—not only for the dispensing of information, which can be done through e-mail, videoconferencing, or memos—but also for the person-to-person interaction that reinforces their connectedness. A collective learning capacity is built as people with similar experiences and responsibilities learn from one another. Through this linkage, the leadership team works collaboratively toward the common goal: the achievement of all students in the community, not just those at each individual school. "The team is the engine that drives the PLC effort. It is difficult to overstate the importance of collaborative teams in the improvement process" (DuFour, DuFour, Eaker, & Karhanek, 2004, p. 3).

Through learning communities, school and district leaders grow professionally for the same reasons that teachers do—if not even more. A principal, frequently the only administrator at a grade span, can be isolated with no colleague at the same level in the district; an example might be a high school principal in a district with only one high school. A school leader, at best, may be one of a small group, such as one of several elementary principals in a district. Thus the support of a PLC expands the group to other school leaders and provides the opportunity to problem solve in a collaborative setting.

Leaders who organize and support teacher learning communities become more effective because of their personal PLC experience (Derrington & Cummings, 2008). Hands-on experience with the joys and challenges of working with a PLC results in increased facilitation skills and a better understanding of teachers' rewards or frustrations when implementing a learning community.

The Knowing-Doing Gap

Leaders have a great deal of knowledge, but there is an inertia that develops when they know too much and do too little, a phenomenon named the "knowing-doing gap" (Pfeffer & Sutton, 1999, p. 21). School leaders create a knowing-doing gap when they implement exemplary staff development practices for teachers at the school but fail to apply the same good practice to themselves. Learning to be an effective school or district leader occurs on the job, in large part. Thus we accrue and create knowledge as we live our work lives in isolation from other leaders. In order to capture this individual learning and expand it to the team, we need to develop a model or method. By so doing, we can close the "knowing-doing" gap and convert knowledge into action.

Consider the Arlington School District in the state of Washington, a district that found a way to create a leadership team PLC. To describe the Arlington experience, I interviewed separately Superintendent Linda Byrnes, high school principal Kurt Criscione, middle school principal Brian Beckley, and elementary principals Kathy Engell and Karl Olson.

THE ARLINGTON LEADERSHIP
PROFESSIONAL LEARNING COMMUNITY

In 2007–08, the Arlington School District served 5,622 students, kindergarten through twelfth grade. The district includes one large high school, a small alternative high school, two middle schools, five elementary schools, and a K–12 home resource school. When the leadership team meets with the superintendent, the group, including principals and assistant principals, numbers sixteen. When the cabinet joins in, the group total is twenty-one.

Leadership team meetings have always been important to the Arlington team. However, like most districts, the agenda often includes information items that could be handled in ways other than using limited face-to-face time. The Arlington principals, eager to dialogue on what they were "actually doing" in their buildings, had limited opportunities to do so. Typically, those exchanges were informal, such as at the elementary principals' voluntary breakfast meetings. A more formal structure with regularly scheduled meeting times and a clear focus was necessary if the principals were to build learning together into their ongoing work. Reflective of this need, principals reported that, after many district meetings, "sidebar conversations" on things of importance to the schools came up spontaneously on their way out of the district office. "We talked about practices and asked each other, 'How do you actually do this?'" reported high school principal Kurt Criscione. It was not that the regular meetings were not important; they just were not sufficient.

Team Staff Development

In the summer of 2007 this inadvertently changed when all the Arlington principals—with the exception of a recent hire—attended a DuFour PLC workshop. The principals talked to each other extensively at the workshop, and these conversations continued when they returned to the district. They discussed what they had learned and how the ideas could be translated into the buildings. "We came back with more questions. We wanted to take advantage of each other's ideas and create a forum," reported elementary principal Karl Olson.

About that same time, the superintendent met with the principals to discuss the upcoming year and to plan meaningful staff development for the team. Principals shared their enthusiasm for the PLC model with the superintendent. They also shared their struggle with attempting to understand the actual specifics when implementing a PLC at the schools. It was at this meeting that the notion of a leadership team PLC emerged. Someone suggested the principals "walk the talk" and act as a PLC themselves. "We thought as a team we could do a book study on the topic and through this structure become like a learning community. We could model for the buildings," middle school principal Brian Beckley reflected in our interview.

Creating the time to learn together was a challenge, because every meeting already had a full agenda and leaders were busy. Principals suggested that some of the already scheduled district meeting time be reallocated to a leadership team PLC. They requested that one of the two weekly hours currently focused on district-driven topics be reallocated to a shared team-learning opportunity. Giving up superintendent-directed district time may have been a hurdle to jump elsewhere, but not in Arlington. "The superintendent saw we were serious about it. She made it happen," elementary principal Kathy Engell acknowledged. Similarly, Superintendent Linda Byrnes reported that, when she saw the principals' passion for this learning opportunity, she quickly agreed to allocate the time. The group decided one hour on the district agenda would be kept clear and "held sacred" for the learning community discussions. "The superintendent supported this change. That was the key—support at the top," Kathy emphasized.

After they had created the time, they chose the book *Learn by Doing* (DuFour, DuFour, Eaker, & Many, 2006) and used district funds to purchase a copy of this book for each team member. "The purpose of the book was to serve as a vehicle to drive the conversation about what we are doing at our buildings," Kurt said. He added that the book was a way to "develop common language, start listening to others, and get our creative juices flowing." They shared ideas on handling school challenges and rewards encountered when forming a PLC in the schools. The team had previously engaged in a book study. While this first study was satisfactory, like any first effort the group attempted to simultaneously learn both a process and the content. The sharing and sense of openness were somewhat limited, due to the "learn-as-you-go" approach.

Following their only previous experience with a book study, the team now had a clearer idea of what was needed to make a new type of dialogue successful. They also had the common knowledge base that attendance at the summer conference had provided. Those principals interviewed agreed all participants in the learning community need a similar knowledge base, and that a book provides a beginning.

The Arlington team had several objectives: they wanted to read a book on their own, apply ideas in the buildings between meetings, and discuss the book and report on their individual results at each meeting. They also agreed that they would each come prepared, which meant reading the assigned chapter and being ready to discuss school implementation examples and questions. During the hour set aside, the team talked specifically about how the text material related to his or her school. The book and each principal's experiences provided the basis for learning. Kurt said, "We ask, 'What are you doing in your building?' We openly share. As a result, we are developing a common language, listening to our successes, and getting ideas from others to implement at our school." Kurt admitted that in the early stages of the PLC questions from others could sound like challenges to the speaker's ideas and convey a negative judgment. However, this potential difficulty was surmounted quickly because the team had built an earlier foundation of trust. "We are willing to ask the tough questions now to get results," Kurt stressed.

Development and Posting of Norms

Some of the Arlington principals reported they felt a little awkward discussing the first chapter of the book and their frustrations in implementing PLCs at the school. Principals are not accustomed to sharing less-than-perfect results in a group that includes bosses as well as peers. Revealing frustrations and shortcomings could be interpreted negatively by peers and "the boss." Thus, it was vitally important that principals felt safe to share openly, and that they feel free from the risk of embarrassment. To create this safe space, it was important for them to develop norms for guiding the group work. Clarity of expectations for behavior and the subsequent accountability to the expectations were discussed when developing norms. After the expectations were developed and agreed on, they were posted in the meeting room and remained there throughout the year. Following are the norms that this team developed:

Book Study Norms

1. Come prepared.

2. Use appropriate humor.

3. Listen, respect, and look for how you can apply information.

4. Use group participation for creating agendas and sticking to them.

5. Support group decisions.

LESSONS LEARNED, POINTS TO PONDER

The Arlington School District PLC experience provides a direction for other leadership teams. Through their story it becomes clear that establishing a leadership team PLC begins by building relationships and altering the hierarchy. Only then is the team able to implement a new type of dialogue that permits learning to become job embedded.

Relationships Precede Revelations

Although there have been changes and turnover in principal leadership, the team builds ongoing support for one another. "We have a pretty good group of administrators who aren't afraid to ask for help. It's a small community. We know each other's warts," Kurt explained. "It isn't just because the team has been together that long. It is that people were hired who are into relationships and are not competitive." He indicated the superintendent would have "a one-on-one conversation" with a team member who did not uphold the group norms.

Arlington values team building and develops trust. In our interview, Karl talked about the opportunities for the group to participate in informal social activities in addition to formal multiday retreats. The district, recognizing the importance of relationships, provides time to make connections between principals and the superintendent. Building relationships and bonding are very important to the Arlington team, and are seen as a step in allowing a PLC to be successful.

Providing the Structure

A school or district leader nowadays has an extraordinarily time-demanding, pressure-filled job. Just keeping on top of the day-to-day activities in the current accountability environment requires intense energy and time. Principals need renewal and are energized by the occasions in which they learn from one another.

I wondered what structures need to be in place to support the development of a learning team of school and district leaders. To answer this question, I examined school learning community concepts that may be applied to district learning teams. Sheppard and Brown (2000) studied the problems encountered when schools become learning organizations. As expected, some of the problems were lack of time, turnover in staff, apathy toward change, and too many initiatives. The most surprising problem to me was that the school staff could not embrace the team leadership concept. The image of the hierarchy was too strong. Some learning teams failed, at least in part, because the principals held reservations or exhibited resistance to sharing power. The researchers also found that the district office directives on different and competing goals and initiatives stifled their efforts and fueled the hierarchical image. Teachers felt bombarded with initiatives from within and from outside the school. Applying these findings to district teams implies that the hierarchy will need to change. All participants must honor the necessary learning curve, and allow time to learn these new behaviors.

Superintendent Becomes a Peer in a PLC

Organizations typically revolve around control: controlling decisions, controlling damage, controlling information, and controlling others. However, complex systems are not controllable, as Peter Senge noted in an interview with Zemke (1999). Senge strongly emphasized team learning and the knowledge, skills, and capabilities that are embedded in the team. The team has the skill within itself to learn. However, to facilitate this learning a superintendent in a PLC needs to be more democratic than autocratic, more supportive than judgmental, and more of a colearner than a solo leader.

Power and authority are hallmarks of bureaucracies and bureaucracies produce compliance. Learning organizations, on the other hand, produce knowledge and are driven by values. A bureaucratic model is incompatible with the learning organization and its capacity to embrace innovations required for continuous improvement (Schlechty, 2006). Leadership in a team-learning environment is not controlling, positional, or directive—it is trusting, sharing, and open.

Mirroring this notion, Superintendent Byrnes said, "I try to keep my mouth shut during the principals' conversations. I learn more about what's going on in instruction at the schools through these dialogues." Principals agree that the superintendent is a "peer" in this process. Furthermore, this hierarchical change is necessary to support open dialogue. It is extremely important, principals report, that when a leadership PLC is formed the conversations take place in a protected, risk-free environment of trust. "If you are opening up, you want to be sure it doesn't get into your evaluation," a principal confided.

Barriers Broken

School districts have "nuts and bolts" items that must be handled to keep the organization functioning smoothly. Thus, giving up a large chunk of meeting time for a PLC decreases time for these other important, but mundane, matters. "Trying to fit the other items into the remaining hour can be a challenge," noted Brian. "It's like teachers say about faculty meetings. They want meetings to be applicable to what's happening in the classroom so it's not *just* nuts and bolts. Principals want meetings at the district to be applicable to what's happening in the building. This is a great tool to start. You'll see people more excited about going to meetings."

Meshing together the wide range of views that K–12 principals bring to a discussion can be a barrier to creating a district PLC. Superintendents frequently hear "that's an elementary issue," or "we don't do that at the middle school." Arlington principals revealed how they broke through this barrier and developed a district viewpoint. "We try to see how we fit into the bigger picture and the dialogue builds empathy," said Karl. "Although I'm elementary, I can get more in-depth in the secondary lives by listening to them." There is also a crossover of ideas. Karl provided an example of how he implemented an idea from middle school into his elementary school. "There's an openness that's developed among us. We realize good ideas can come from all levels." As Karl explained, because principals can feel isolated on the job, "It helps to know everyone is going through challenges and that we all have our successes too."

Apprehensiveness about sharing openly can be a barrier to PLC discussion. "You don't want to come across as a know-it-all or ignorant," one of the principals remarked. It is important to communicate and continuously convey that this is a safe, nonjudgmental environment. Restating and revisiting the norms is one way to refocus on purpose and process.

The size of a learning group matters; twenty or more is large when an entire leadership team is assembled. The team needs a focused agenda or else dialogue can ramble, or be dominated by a few people. Recognizing this negative potential, Kurt indicated a need for group regulation. "We became pretty good self-monitors." He also observed that principals become adept at reading body language and thus kept the group on task when the conversation went sideways.

A Different Dialogue Develops

One aspect of learning in a professional development team is dialogue—and not just any dialogue, but deep reflective open conversations about things that matter. Creating a community of learners is not a program, but a process. It is a way of understanding and growing, both individually and as a team. Conversation is the tool used to facilitate communication conducive to this learning process (Bierema, 1999).

The Arlington PLC thrives because of the powerful dialogue. "We have rich conversations, and it will only get better," Kathy confirmed. "You have to open yourself up to new ideas to benefit," Brian added. "No one feels they're perfect. I am comfortable saying, 'This is something I missed the boat on.'" Creativity comes from this open dialogue and the sharing of an abundance of ideas. "After the meetings, I have a list of things I want to do," Kurt reflected. "The only barrier is time. I wonder how I will get this done when there is so much to do."

When asked if anything about the dialogue surprised her, Kathy said, "I'm surprised at how positive and rich the conversations are and how they can impact us on a daily basis in our schools."

All agree that developing dialogue skill is a good first step in forming a leadership team PLC. "We're in start-up and talking about collaboration time and how to help our teams. The conversation has potential to impact us; we're talking," Kathy said. Brian echoed the feelings of the others when he said, "I enjoy our meetings. I know we'll have meaningful conversations, and I'll take some ideas from it." Kathy added, "It's worth our time and effort. We share, we learn. Rather than a feeling of going it alone, I walk away and feel that I'm part of a team."

A Curriculum for Leadership Team Learning

- Build the belief. Busy principals and superintendents have to be convinced that the time spent in team learning pays dividends. Provide reasons why team learning is important.
- Adjust the attitudes. A foundation of trust and supportive actions is required for collaborative team work. Take steps to assist the team to share successes and failures in a risk-free environment.
- Create the conditions. The foundation for success includes providing the time to learn and a flattened hierarchy. Reflect on your team philosophy and whether or not you can relinquish authority and play on a level field.
- Determine the prerequisite skills. A team needs interpersonal skills and the ability to dialogue constructively. Discuss and develop norms to guide positive team interactions.
- Celebrate continuous improvement. No team is perfect in its initial effort in any new learning. Gather feedback and data on group progress and seek to improve your own performance.

TAKE-AWAY MESSAGE

Provide districtwide leadership and a role model for schools by engaging in continuous learning as a superintendent-principal team. Begin by examining exemplary staff development practices at the schools and reflect on the potential applications to the leadership team. One strategy is to develop a learning team of leaders by applying the PLC concept. Lessons learned at the Arlington School District illustrate that relationships, structures, time, and a set of specific skills should be addressed and considered to become a team that continuously grows in its capacity to learn and to lead.

CLOSING IN ON KEY CONCEPTS

- PLCs increase collective competence.
- Principals and their superintendent can become a community of learners.
- Support for a leadership learning community requires the superintendent to act as a peer and colearner.
- Relationships built on trust promote effective dialogue in the PLC.
- A critical element is the ability to engage in open conversation in a risk-free environment.

EXTENDING YOUR THINKING

1. Are the prerequisite skills and conditions that enable leaders to learn together present in your leadership team?

2. How can you adapt the Arlington School District process to your own leadership team needs?

3. What barriers will your team need to address to be an effective community of learners?

The Principal's Perspective

8

Perfecting Principal Performance

*Helping principals achieve their goals, and the goals they served,
was essential to me as superintendent. When they were building
capacity, I knew the organization was growing and improving
as well.*

—Dr. Gene Sharratt, Director, Superintendent
Certification Program, Washington State University

Principals are coming into their profession better prepared than ever before. Most have completed rigorous master's degrees and principal certification programs, engaged in substantial internships, and produced extensive portfolios that address tough school administrator standards. Will these laudatory accomplishments ensure school leadership success? Probably not, given the complexities associated with running a school—ever-shifting accountability directives, onerous student assessment requirements, voluminous service requests from staff and clients, dwindling budgets, crisis-level discipline problems, and a complicated web of state and federal regulations—not to mention personnel responsibilities such as hiring, training, supervising, motivating, and evaluating. This may include admonishing or dismissing staff members—risky endeavors requiring extensive time, up-to-the-minute legal knowledge, and superior communication skills. So no matter how well prepared new principals might be, superintendents must orchestrate activities that perfect performance over time. This begins by getting principals off to a solid start.

ENSURING SUCCESS

Shortly after my twenty-ninth birthday I stepped through the door of the first school I would lead. I approached this endeavor with such unbridled confidence my memory of this precipitous event thirty years later leaves me breathless. I came armed with a newly acquired administrator's certificate, a freshly signed contract, and a bundle of unidentified school keys issued by my superintendent's secretary. I had not been given a job description, however, or an orientation to my school, a mentor, or any kind of "new principal" induction. Given that I had completed the briefest of administrative practicums, my notion about what a principal did from day to day was almost nonexistent. My confidence faded quickly as I confronted the never-ending challenges associated with leading a school. That I survived my first year as principal is as much a testament to the patience of my faculty as it is to the resilience of youth.

Flashing forward to a different school district and community, I confidently stepped through the door of another school I would lead—but this time my self-assuredness was well founded. This was not just because I had gained experience as a principal, but also because my new superintendent's game plan for new hires is second to none. Superintendent Doug Nelson, my new boss, leaves nothing to chance. His orientation for principals—experienced or not—includes a wide array of activities: tours of the school district and community, an induction seminar, an administrative retreat (which Doug calls an "advance" because, in his words, "We *never* retreat!"), visitations with teachers and students, and meetings with district-level administrators and the departing principal. Sound good? You bet! But there are additional ways Doug nurtures new hires: he schedules an in-depth briefing before the school year starts, requires the principal to prepare a detailed entry plan, and conducts a thorough internal review about six months into the school year. What follows are descriptions of these supportive activities and the payoff for principals.

The Briefing

Doug began my orientation soon after my contract was signed with a briefing he provided himself. This personal attention initiated the bonding process that is vital for sound superintendent-principal relationships. First, I heard the story of my school—its history, successes, and setbacks. He provided enough information to get me started, but not so much that I would walk into my school with preconceived notions about the faculty and families I would serve. I learned next more about my superintendent's "expectation of excellence," an expectation that had been evident throughout the hiring process.

My superintendent's mission for principals was threefold: put students first, be data driven when gauging school success, and bring a high-quality performance to every endeavor. I left the briefing excited to get started, with a strong sense of purpose and a firm commitment to my new boss. In *The Hidden Leader*, Dale Brubaker and Larry Coble capture the power of visionary leadership:

> The visionary leader creates conditions under which others feel inspired and committed to something greater than themselves. Visionary leaders are able to literally "paint a picture" with their words, which leave stakeholders with an understanding of purpose and direction. (2005, p. 6)

EXPECTATION OF EXCELLENCE

Principals' professional growth begins with hiring—a rigorous process that involves multiple steps. There's an individual interview with the superintendent and a team interview with administrative, teacher, and parent representatives. Each candidate makes a presentation to the interview team, reviews a videotaped lesson which is followed by a post-conference with the teacher, and writes an essay. Our hiring process sets an *expectation of excellence* for candidates. They know they have been through a rigorous process and that I *expect* them to be at an equally high level in what they do. (Superintendent Doug Nelson)

The Entry Plan

I also left the superintendent's briefing with my first assignment—to write an entry plan. This involved outlining step by step how I would transition to my new school. Goals, activities, and timelines were to be included covering five essential areas: instructional leadership, school-community interactions, school management, school and staff evaluation, and professional development. I had always begun a job with a lengthy "to do" list but the entry plan was more comprehensive; it would ensure that important people, programs, policies, and procedures were not missed. The power of entry plans (Resource D) is highlighted in the Q & A that follows.

SUPERINTENDENT NELSON Q & A

Cathie: How do entry plans help new hires?

Doug: With a good entry plan principals get to know their buildings quickly and establish relationships, which is the *most* important aspect of a good start. They need to quickly learn their school's culture, norms, informal power structure, challenges, and opportunities. They need to know the "sacred cows" so they don't "step in it" inadvertently.

(Continued)

(Continued)

Cathie: Entry plan activities produce valuable information. What's next for the principal?

Doug: To identify challenges and formulate goals. Entry plans provide a qualitative way for principals to gather data and start work on critical issues.

Cathie: You encourage staff interviews. Why are these important?

Doug: Because staff will *always* tell principals about problems. Later, when principals address these problems, they have positioned themselves to be effective in the eyes of their staff.

Cathie: Sounds like a valuable payoff for *any* administrator.

Doug: Strong leaders know the values, wishes, commitment, and expertise of their followers. The best way to find out is to ask. In the asking comes the *power.* Asking also honors people and sends a strong message of caring. Relationships are formed and it's through strong relationships that change is made and accomplishments occur.

The entry plan helped me get up to speed quickly. What came next was equally valuable—an internal review.

The Internal Review

About six months into the job, Doug stopped by my school to schedule an internal review. He would personally interview every one of my staff members about my performance, take notes about perceived strengths and weaknesses, and then share this information with me. I was taken aback by this proposal—I had read about "360-degree feedback" where leaders are evaluated by colleagues, supervisors, and direct reports (Brubaker & Coble, 2005), but no previous superintendent had done anything like this before. How would I fare? My school was just getting on board with school improvement initiatives and change comes hard. I knew that my persistent nudge in this direction was unsettling to some teachers. Could my boss "filter" teacher concerns in the light of the difficult work my staff and I had begun?

On the day of the review, Doug spent a full morning and afternoon ensconced in the school's conference room interviewing classified and certificated staff members. He asked each person just four questions, all of them open ended (see the box on page 93).

INTERNAL REVIEW QUESTIONS

How has the school year gone?

What are the principal's strengths?

How could the principal improve performance?

What should next year's goals be?

The internal review yielded staff comments that were affirming, and suggestions that led to goal updates. Most beneficial, however, were the stimulating "postreview" conversations that I had with my boss. As noted in the following interview, internal reviews provide a rewarding evaluative experience.

SUPERINTENDENT NELSON Q & A

Cathie: How do you orchestrate internal reviews to support principals over time?

Doug: The reviews are completed early in the principal's career and ideally are repeated every five years. In my current district we have twenty-four principals so a team of central office administrators gets involved. The team visits a school and interviews as many of the staff, classified and certificated as possible. The interviews are open ended and focus on how well the school and principal are doing. An objective survey is also administered. The principal's immediate supervisor compiles the qualitative information from the interviews and the quantitative data from the surveys and develops feedback "themes" to share.

Cathie: What's the benefit for principals?

Doug: Internal reviews are done in a manner to encourage professional growth. They acknowledge the talents of the principal and identify what, if anything, needs to be strengthened. They have been affirming while also causing significant change.

Superintendent Nelson's personal attention, coupled with briefings, entry plans, and internal reviews, provides a solid framework for principal success.

PERFECTING PERFORMANCE

After the dust has settled and new principals are well into their jobs, does high productivity and quality performance automatically follow? Not without attention. There are two paths to peak performance; the first concerns the principal's responsibility to be self-motivated and self-directed. Charlotte Rafferty, a National Distinguished Principal from Florida, calls this "an intrinsic motivation to learn." The second path to success is the supportive way superintendents keep principals thriving.

The Principal's Responsibility

Awhile back, I joined a principal team that included a team member who was coasting. This principal could have been the poster child for "status quo." He had not initiated an innovative project in recent memory, read a professional book from start to finish in decades, or engineered change of any significance in his school. It was frustrating working alongside this wastrel, and even more frustrating witnessing the negative impact his nonperformance had on students and teachers. Fortunately, this idler was eventually replaced with a principal who was professionally "on fire." Spirited principals make a difference in their schools, make those around them aspire to a higher level of performance, and make school districts better. Professionally adept leaders share the following qualities:

- *Informed:* They know their field and stay current regarding educational research, instructional practice, and assessment.
- *Being Teachers:* They share their knowledge with others through modeling, teaching, mentoring, and leading substantive projects.
- *Competent:* They know and adhere to professional performance standards, such as the Standards for School Leaders developed by the Interstate School Leaders Licensure Consortium (CCSSO, 1996).
- *Being Rule Followers:* They demonstrate strong professional ethics and are attentive to district, state, and federal requirements.
- *Being Change Agents:* They refuse to accept the status quo. They stay on the cutting edge by finding new ways to improve their schools and themselves.
- *Diligent:* They take pride in working long, hard, and well.
- *Persistent:* They relentlessly pursue formidable goals.
- *Collaborative:* They bring a team approach to the challenges at hand.
- *Successful:* They measure success by the achievement of students, the effectiveness of teachers, and the satisfaction of clients.

School Leadership
Performance Standard Sources

- *Interstate School Leaders Licensure Consortium: Standards for School Leaders* by Council of Chief State School Officers (1996)
- *Leading Learning Communities: Standards for What Principals Should Know and Be Able to Do* by National Association of Elementary School Principals (2001)
- *Principal Leadership: Applying the New Educational Leadership Constituent Council (ELCC) Standards* by Elaine L. Wilmore (2002)
- *School Leadership that Works: From Research to Results* by Robert J. Marzano, Timothy Waters, & Brian A. McNulty (2005)

Competent principals are also voracious readers of professional books, journals, and educational Web sites; they attend trainings that keep them up to date, take on growth-provoking assignments, write goals that align with rigorous school leadership performance standards, and serve on professional committees and boards.

Learning by Leading

Experiencing the leadership loop of president elect, president, and past president of the Nebraska Association of Elementary School Principals provided missing pieces to my leadership puzzle. The opportunity to be among "leaders of leaders" and to observe their approaches to problem solving, networking, and interacting with other professionals was truly enlightening. It drove home that to be *really* effective, you must possess skills in many areas, skills which set you apart from others in similar positions and make you the "go-to person."

I also learned from serving with principals from a wide variety of schools that being a highly successful leader *always* comes down to the person—not the school or the position held.

In education we develop a bunker mentality over time and lose sight of the options we have to do what we do *better*. Being involved in my state association broadened my horizons through interaction with others. In turn, I brought fresh insights and ideas back to my school and administrative team and we made changes in how we do business. Service at the state level was the biggest professional growth opportunity of my career. (Mark Murphy, National Distinguished Principal, Nebraska)

Regardless of the superintendent, proficient principals learn—but they learn more from superintendents who engineer their professional development.

The Superintendent's Responsibility

I once worked for a superintendent who was highly competent technically but who was also professionally aloof. There were no discussions about his vision for our school district, his mission for the principals' schools, or topical educational issues. Communication was limited to the nuts and bolts of running school. Adrift professionally, his principals chose the course they would follow to improve their schools. Not surprisingly, at evaluation time there was a startling disconnect between the superintendent's appraisal of performance and the principals' own assessments. His commentary, although favorable, was out of sync with actual accomplishments, which impeded meaningful discussion about professional practice. I eventually took a job in a different school district, which offered me a challenging assignment coupled with the chance to work for a well-respected superintendent. It was this boss who introduced me to the power of a strong superintendent-principal relationship and a meaningful supervision and evaluation process.

Supervising and Evaluating Effectively

Many principals picture paperwork when they think about their own performance evaluations. They picture documents hurriedly prepared by an overworked superintendent each spring and quickly signed and dismissed by principals more concerned about closing school successfully than about their own accomplishments. Unfortunately, in too many districts the responsibility for principals' evaluations rests solely with the superintendent, the year-end performance report is more ritualistic than significant, and the final evaluation occurs at such a frantic time of the school year that little attention is given to it.

Savvy superintendents and principals bring much more to the supervision-evaluation process. They see it as an ongoing dialogue between the superintendent and principal, punctuated by relevant evaluative activities throughout the year.

These evaluative activities include codeveloping the principal's annual

---

HELPING PRINCIPALS STRETCH

When I was a superintendent, I met with each principal at the beginning of each year to assist in the development of a professional growth plan. This plan was to set "stretching" goals—both personal and professional—that went beyond regular job requirements. These goals were not included in formative or summative evaluations unless completed. I did not want principals to *not* attempt growth out of fear of evaluation.

I met with my principals four times a year to monitor and support their "stretch" goals. My task was to encourage, recommend, support, and provide resources. It was paramount to build a relationship where I could assist principals in building their capacity to grow, to lead, and to encourage teachers to become leaders within their classrooms and their school. It was my experience that when principals "stretched," teachers and schools stretched. (Dr. Gene Sharratt, Director, Superintendent Certification Program, Washington State University) goal plan; meeting on a regular basis (ideally, monthly) to discuss progress; analyzing student achievement data; coordinating school self-studies; surveying students, staff, and parents; completing school leadership self-assessments; and preparing performance status reports. When it comes time for the final evaluation—hopefully after the crush of closing school— it becomes the responsibility of both the superintendent and the principal to review accomplishments and assess performance.

Principal improvement takes time but is vital: principal performance impacts teacher performance, which ultimately affects student achievement (Marzano, Waters, & McNulty, 2005). Billie Jo Drake, a National Distinguished Principal from Kansas, provides an example: "One of my superintendents would routinely critique my observation and evaluation documents. This attention allowed me to do a better job of helping teachers to improve *their* practices." Principal Charlotte Rafferty sums up the connection between principal and teacher performance nicely: "When principals are supported professionally they can train their *own* teams to be strong and smart."

Engineering Growth

Principals benefit from superintendents who are strong supervisors and evaluators. These superintendents engineer principals' professional growth by implementing activities that keep their school leaders current, competent, and committed.

❧

SUPERINTENDENT AND TEACHER

About ten years ago a new superintendent arrived who initiated professional development for all staff members. His workshops covered multiple intelligences, brain-based instruction, and cooperative learning. This was our district's first experience with a superintendent who was a *teacher*. The superintendent really knew his material and his lessons were invigorating and challenging. As an experienced school administrator, I appreciated my superintendent's knowledge and energy.

He also challenged each of his principals to develop new programs. Mine was a multiage approach for students in Grades 1–3. With the help of a facilitating teacher—which is something he also instituted—and a great staff, our program merited a Best Practices Award from the New Jersey Department of Education.

This superintendent knew how to motivate principals and staff to explore new ideas. He was a true leader and teacher! (Louis DellaBarca, National Distinguished Principal, New Jersey)

TEN WAYS SUPERINTENDENTS ENHANCE PRINCIPAL PERFORMANCE

Implementing Professional Standards:	Helping principals put state- and national-level performance standards into effect
Teaching:	Sharing leadership expertise and new developments in the field of education
Engaging:	Creating stimulating meeting agendas that include a strong professional development component (such as informative book studies), discussions about educational practice, and opportunities to share leadership successes
Teaming to Learn:	Taking principals to noteworthy conferences and collaboratively identifying ways to utilize new concepts and skills
Challenging:	Stimulating principal growth by encouraging risk taking, setting ambitious goals, and encouraging leadership work at the regional, state, and national levels
Affirming:	Privately and publicly recognizing principals' accomplishments
Collaborating:	Working with principals to set goals, reach objectives, and solve problems
Supporting:	Providing funds for books, training, national conferences, and innovative projects
Monitoring:	Requesting substantive principal goal plans (Resource E) and monitoring accomplishments
Coevaluating:	Involving principals in self-evaluation, self-reflection, student-assessment analysis, and goal-attainment reviews

———— ✀ ————

ON TAKING RISKS

Most superintendents don't like their principals to make waves because the backlash often splashes into their offices. My superintendent always wore rain gear. He encouraged us to take risks for kids and to think outside the box. (David Root, National Distinguished Principal, Ohio)

Success does not spring from every action taken: rather, it is the skill of implementation that makes the difference. So I quizzed Superintendent Nelson, whose exemplary orientation activities were highlighted earlier, about book studies. They make up a vital part of his principal development program and, as one might expect, they become a powerful tool in the hands of an artful superintendent.

SUPERINTENDENT NELSON Q & A

Cathie: How have book studies helped your administrative team?

Doug: Three years ago I had all administrators read *Good to Great* by Jim Collins (2001). The next year we read *Good to Great and the Social Sectors* (Collins, 2005), a monograph about adapting the concepts from *Good to Great* to public sector organizations. We had developed an ambitious strategic plan that we had difficulty implementing and needed a means to pull administrators together. We needed a common direction and alignment. *Good to Great* became a wonderful advanced organizer around which we developed a common vocabulary and approach. Adding the social sector piece helped some administrators make the business connection to schools. The book studies helped get us on the same page.

Cathie: I like the way you use book studies to strengthen your team. What came next?

Doug: This year we read *Whatever It Takes* by DuFour, DuFour, Eaker, and Karhanek (2004). *Whatever It Takes* contributed to the evolution of becoming focused and aligned.

Cathie: Your book selections are very intentional.

Doug: The selections were made to meet the needs of our organization at that moment and to help us move forward *together*. They gave us a shared vision about possibilities.

BOOK STUDY TOP TEN PICKS

- *Building Smart Teams: A Roadmap to High Performance* by Carol A. Beatty and Brenda A. Barker Scott (2004)
- *Change Forces: The Sequel* by Michael Fullan (1999)
- *Good to Great: Why Some Companies Make the Leap—and Others Don't* by Jim Collins (2001)
- *How to Deal With Teachers Who Are Angry, Troubled, Exhausted, or Just Plain Confused* by Elaine K. McEwan (2005)
- *Leading for Results: Transforming Teaching, Learning, and Relationships in Schools* by Dennis Sparks (2005)
- *Lessons Learned: Shaping Relationships and the Culture of the Workplace* by Roland Barth (2003)
- *The Hidden Leader: Leadership Lessons on the Potential Within* by Dale L. Brubaker and Larry D. Coble (2005)
- *Primal Leadership: Realizing the Power of Emotional Intelligence* by Daniel Goleman, Richard Boyatzis, Annie McKee (2002)
- *Research on Educational Innovations* by Arthur K. Ellis (2005)
- *10 Traits of Highly Effective Principals: From Good to Great Performance* by Elaine K. McEwan (2003)

PRINCIPAL PERFORMANCE IMPACT

Perfecting performance is a gift that superintendents bring to their principal teams: a gift that comes in a variety of packaging—from book studies to precious dollars for national conferences, from collaboration time with colleagues to individual self-studies, from district awards to a simple but sincere pat on the back.

Perfecting performance also includes the kind of behind-the-scenes support described in the reflection that follows. Principal Kari Henderson-Burke has been fortunate to work with a superintendent who has become her best coach: "He believes that *every* topic is important. To every question or situation, no matter how miniscule or mundane, he has been a consistent and cheerful responder."

SUPERINTENDENT AND CHEERLEADER

Under my current superintendent I was nominated for and received the National Distinguished Principal of the Year Award. My school also earned the A+ School Award. When each of these recognitions were celebrated, the superintendent came to school with pins and cakes for me and my staff. What fun we had!

My staff had always known they were great, but having the superintendent's recognition was even better! (Jackie Doer, Principal, National Distinguished Principal, Arizona)

MY TRANSFORMATIONAL JOURNEY

A classroom teacher for ten years, I spent only one year as a Teacher on Special Assignment before becoming a principal. Even with excellent training, varied internship experiences, and a strong desire to grow into the position, my superintendent understood that I needed support in my transformation from teacher to principal.

Initially, he supported my journey by helping me clarify my new role. During my first year, for example, I set a well-intended goal of increasing math scores—a teacher's goal. Through questioning and conversation, he helped me reframe the goal to supporting *teachers'* efforts to increase math achievement through improved instruction. Acknowledging the intent of my original goal, he subtly helped me shift my responsibility from improving math to improving teachers.

Later my superintendent helped me use conflict as an improvement tool. During a faculty disagreement over an action I had taken, he validated my professionalism by saying, "Your decision was sound and reasonable. This is what we pay you to do." He then asked me to use the conflict to improve and strengthen relationships with teachers. Through his guidance, the conflict became an opportunity to build trust.

My superintendent also understood the importance of professional relationships in assisting growth. He has cultivated a collaborative, supportive district leadership team.

Each team meeting, planning session, and training encourages collegial relationships and reminds me that I am a part of a professional learning community.

Now, mid-way through my second year as a principal, I recognize how skillfully and patiently my superintendent has taught me to be a principal. The journey is not complete, but it is a journey well begun. (Principal Kari Henderson-Burke, Washington)

Transformation is an apt term for the change that takes place in principals as they gain experience, knowledge, and skills. As a bonus, the process principals engage in as they mature professionally also benefits superintendents.

PERFECTING SUPERINTENDENT PERFORMANCE

"School is not a place for important people who do not need to learn and unimportant people who do, quipped Roland Barth, founder of the Harvard Principal Center (Sennett, 2004, p. 2). Superintendent Doug Nelson takes this epigram to heart by leading by example; in a recent interview he shared this insight: "When you expect high performance from principals you must have the same high expectations for yourself. Principals will continue to perform at very high levels when the superintendent is also performing well. High level expectations start with the leader. Superintendents are being watched both internally and externally and they must be the best possible—that performance sets the tone."

LEADING BY EXAMPLE

I get the most out of active learning—going to trainings that provide information about new programs or approaches. I attend seminars sponsored by the Oregon Leadership Network, for example, and they provide a great opportunity to learn and grow.

I also read journals and trade magazines—skimming the contents for articles of interest. If they have merit I circulate the articles to my administrators. If I find a powerful book I read it. Those are the ones that have become our book studies.

Colleagues have always been a great source of professional growth—talking with them, bouncing off ideas, asking questions, and seeking advice. Most recently I have used an executive coach, a practice in business that is finding its way into education. My coach has helped me address issues, define problems, and seek solutions. I am now in training to serve as an executive coach for others. Being a superintendent is a lonely job. Unlike principals, the superintendent has no one at a peer level. Superintendents need someone in whom they can confide and seek guidance. An executive coach provides excellent support! (Superintendent Doug Nelson, Oregon)

Superior superintendents are deliberate when they model professional growth for their principals. They not only engage in the same kinds of professional development, but also include their principals in these activities. As superintendents engage their administrators in enlightening book studies, take their teams to powerful leadership institutes, or arrange team meetings with specialized consultants, powerful discussions take place and collective insights are formed. These shared experiences strengthen everyone's professional performance and inspire greater effort. There is a performance-enhancing "connection that raises the level of motivation . . . in *both* the leader and the follower" (Northouse, 2007, p. 170, italics mine). As superintendents transform principals they transform themselves.

TAKE-AWAY MESSAGE

Principals need a superintendent who makes their professional development a priority—not only at the start of their careers, but also throughout their professional lives. Improved performance positively impacts all stakeholders: students, teachers, administrative team, and superintendent.

CLOSING IN ON KEY CONCEPTS

For the Superintendent

- No matter how well prepared or experienced new principal hires might at the onset, plan activities that get them off to a solid start.
- Orientation activities like briefings, entry plans, and internal reviews help new principals find direction, learn their role and responsibilities, and set goals for their school.
- Incorporate growth activities that perfect principal performance over time.
- Keep administrative teams thriving through ongoing professional development.

For the Principal

- Take control of your own learning.
- Write goal plans that align with school and district goals, state school-improvement initiatives, and professional standards for school leaders.
- Contribute to the professional growth of fellow principals, the administrative team, and your superintendent.

EXTENDING YOUR THINKING

For Principals

1. What plans have you made for your professional development?

2. In what ways have you contributed to the growth of fellow principals? Your administrative team? Your superintendent?

3. How will you let your superintendent know about your professional development needs?

For Superintendents

1. What steps do you take to prepare new principals for job challenges?

2. How do you support the growth of principals throughout their careers?

3. When you implement activities to strengthen principals, are you also growing? In what ways?

Conclusion

Leadership Teaming spotlighted the vital parts played by superintendents and principals in their school districts, roles that have become increasingly complex. Responsibilities have skyrocketed, while social and political forces challenge every administrator's ability to provide a high-quality public education. No matter how knowledgeable, dynamic, or influential a superintendent or principal may be individually, neither can operate independently. Job responsibilities are great and working relationships intricately interwoven. Both superintendent and principal successes lie in a team approach.

Intuitively we understand the importance of team. Every candidate for an administrative position gives the standard response, "I'm a team player," at least once during an interview, and wise selection committee members nod approvingly. However, we all know that teaming effectively is "easier said than done." To team successfully, principals must understand the superintendent's mission, the forces at play in the district environment, the dynamic role of the administrative team, and their part in the leadership mix. At the same time, superintendents must craft a team that is cohesive while incorporating the individual missions, varied talents, and unique perspectives of every principal. For both superintendents and principals, teamwork requires an understanding of how successful teams function, respect for the unique contributions of individual team members, and a willingness to embrace the challenges associated with effective teaming.

This book describes pathways to team success. We close by revisiting the four themes that guided our work and highlighting key concepts for the superintendents who desire a high-functioning team, for principals who will undertake the steps leading to team effectiveness, and for all the team players who know that teamwork is a delicate interplay of one's professional expertise, collaborative skills, ethical sense, and interpersonal flair.

LEADERSHIP TEAMING KEY CONCEPTS

Leadership Teaming

- Administrative success is not an individual pursuit, but rather a team endeavor.
- Strong relationships build strong teams.
- Optimistic outlooks benefit team members and team effectiveness.

Leadership Qualities

- Instructional leadership is a vital skill for every school leader.
- Well-developed interpersonal skills are critical for team success.
- Competence, caring, and commitment support team development.

Leadership Team Essentials

- Open and frequent communication builds trusting, enduring relationships.
- Trust underlies healthy superintendent-principal relationships.
- Supportive superintendents earn principals' confidence and commitment.

Leadership Learning

- Savvy superintendents nurture their principals.
- Competent principals take control of their own learning, but learn more from superintendents who orchestrate their professional development.
- Strong teams are a community of learners whose members openly share knowledge, experience, and wisdom.

Healthy team dynamics transforms an assortment of individuals into a cohesive group that grows in competence and prepares the team to realize its mission. This was our experience as coauthors for *Leadership Teaming.* Our book sprung several years ago from leisurely musings nourished by a passion for our topic and a healthy dose of optimism. We were experienced administrators and knew we had a lot to share. As a bonus, each of us had published before—articles, book reviews, and research reports. We wondered, naïvely, if writing a book together could be that hard. We soon learned that moving from reverie to reality would take all the laudatory attributes and every team-enhancing skill explored in our book.

Carving out time for research, collaboration, and writing was the first challenge. We each had family obligations and full-time jobs that seemed at times to be all consuming. Setting shared goals and deadlines was the obvious answer, but creating a plan is easier than executing it. Setbacks had to be openly discussed and our commitment to the project periodically renewed.

Collaboration was another hurdle. We lived in separate cities and kept different schedules, which hampered face-to-face communication. When we did get together, hammering out agreements regarding themes, topics, research sources, and stories took time and patience. Listening respectfully to each other's ideas was critical, as was a willingness to compromise in order to move forward.

Maintaining a positive, supportive relationship was also imperative. Remarkably, we had bravely agreed to critique each other's work. This required trust and a fair amount of tact. This was especially true when one of us took a bold approach that did not pan out. We mentored one another and, over time, became each other's best writing coach.

Finally, there were times when we became deeply discouraged: We had run into a roadblock—a computer glitch, a lost reference, or a concept we were failing to capture in words. We experienced anxious moments from the enormous effort that goes into producing a book—endless tinkering with content, multiple manuscript deadlines, and mind-boggling production details. We wondered if we could keep up, hold up, and measure up. We helped each other through these difficult times with offers of help and words of encouragement.

Leadership Teaming became a reality because we brought to this project the same attitudes and skills needed by an effective superintendent-principal team. With this in mind, we hope our book helps other teams take heart when times are tough, rescue each other when team members falter, and stay true to their vision.

Resources

RESOURCE A: CODE-BUILDING EXERCISE 1

Team Members From Hell

Think back on your career and to the many relationships you have had with superintendents, personnel directors, business managers, program directors, elementary and secondary principals, and administrative support staff. Are there supervisors and colleagues who are forever etched in your memory because they caused you untold grief, made you furious, provoked sleepless nights, or drove you nuts? What was it about these irksome individuals that set them apart? For the next eight minutes, write about these team members from hell. Who were they? How did they conduct business? What did they say or not say, do or not do?

Sharing

Describe the actions and attributes of your "team members from hell." What can we learn from their misbehaviors?

109

RESOURCE B: CODE-BUILDING EXERCISE 2

Please review the Administrative Code of Ethics and Collaboration that has been provided. It contains expectations that, if observed, might protect you from adverse team members. Follow the steps outlined below.

STEP 1. Read then rate the value of *each* expectation using the key provided.

+ = Important to a well-functioning administrative team

− = Not vital

? = Unsure of importance

STEP 2. Is anything missing? Jot down any suggestions below.

STEP 3. Be prepared to talk about your ratings and recommendations.

STEP 4. Please turn your notes in to your facilitator. Thank you!

RESOURCE C: CODE REVIEW ACTIVITY

Note: Each team should be a mix of elementary-, secondary-, and district-level administrators.

Teams

Team 1 _____

Team 2 _____

Team 3 _____

Team 4 _____

Team 5 _____

Team Task

Your team will be given one of the expectations from our Code of Ethics and Collaboration. Your job is to create a skit that demonstrates a violation of that expectation.

Planning Time: 10–15 minutes

Next Step

As each team performs its skit, try to identify which code is being violated.

RESOURCE D: PRINCIPAL ENTRY PLAN

Cathie E. West, Principal

Instructional Leadership

Goal: Prepare to serve as an instructional leader by becoming acquainted with staff, curriculum, assessment results, school improvement plans, and resources.

Time line: July–August

- Review previous school improvement plans, site council minutes, and student achievement results.

- Read subject area curriculum guides and identify core and supplementary instructional materials.

- Learn about the policies and procedures governing curriculum development and instructional materials selection.

- Identify local and regional professional development opportunities for classified and certificated staff.

- Review the instructional budget allocations, including pertinent grants.

- Meet with district instructional leaders to learn about program policies and procedures: superintendent, director of curriculum and instruction, and Title I and special education directors.

School-Community Interactions

Goal: Initiate communication with school and district staff, students and parents, and community agencies.

Time line: July–September

- Provide staff with informational bulletins and e-mail updates throughout the summer.

- Interview district administrators and coordinators regarding roles, responsibilities, and services: superintendent, director of fiscal services, director of curriculum and instruction, facilities management director, food services supervisor, and transportation director.

- Meet with other principals to get acquainted, gain insights, and share goals.

- Interview every certificated and classified member and survey staff regarding school strengths, weaknesses, and goals.

- Organize a staff "get acquainted" BBQ prior to the start of school.

- Send a letter of introduction to students and their parents or guardians.

- Meet with the PTA or PTO president to plan for the upcoming school year.

- Meet with school board members regarding goals and expectations.

- Meet with social service agency directors about available services for school families.

- Create opportunities to meet students and share information about yourself (e.g., create an "all about me" bulletin board in the front hall, schedule an assembly, and visit classrooms).

School Management

Goal: Become informed about school operation and management essentials.

Time line: July–August

- Meet with the former principal to learn about the school improvement plan, master calendar, school schedule, summer programs, staff vacancies, security procedures, and other relevant information.

- Review school files, including historical records, bulletins, newsletters, personnel documents, discipline records, special education individual education plans, and student medical protocols.

- Organize your office, files, and reference materials.

- Confer with the personnel director about vacancies and read the personnel policy manual to learn job posting requirements and hiring procedures.

- Meet with the executive director of curriculum and instruction to inquire about curriculum projects, computer services, the school database system, and staff inservice opportunities.

- Meet with the special education director, the school psychologist, and the resource room teacher to learn about referral processes, testing policies, counseling services, and programs for special needs children.

- Read the classified and certificated union contracts and introduce yourself to the presidents and to your school's union representatives.

School and Staff Evaluation

Goal: Become acquainted with staff and principal evaluation processes.

Time line: July–August

- Review previous school evaluations, such as "self-studies" and parent surveys.

- Gather and review student achievement results (e.g., school, district, and state assessment data).

- Review certificated and classified evaluation policies and procedures.

- Read the certificated and classified evaluations for the past two years.

- Inquire about the principal evaluation process.

Professional Development

Goal: Prepare short-term and long-range school and principal goals.

Time line: August–October

- Complete your entry plan and review accomplishments with the superintendent.

- Compile the input from staff interviews and surveys and share with the superintendent and staff.

- Involve staff in setting school goals based on interview and survey results and student achievement data.

- Prepare principal goals covering: instructional leadership, interactions, management, evaluation, and professional development.

RESOURCE E: PRINCIPAL PROFESSIONAL GOAL PLAN

Cathie E. West, Principal

	Time Line	Completion Indicators
Instructional Leadership		
Complete the ten-trait audit for highly effective schools developed by Elaine *McEwan (2008), and involve the learning improvement team in analyzing results.	By October 31	Survey results and analysis report
Prepare, with teacher and specialist input, the school year's school improvement plan. Include goals and activities that reflect the 10-trait audit results, last spring's Washington Assessment of Student Learning (WASL) results, and Washington's "Nine Characteristics of Effective Schools (Washington State Office of Superintendent of Public Instruction n.d.).	By November 30	School improvement plan and activity completion report
Increase student achievement in reading, mathematics, writing, and science. Track progress using classroom-based, schoolwide, and state assessments.	September–June	Monitor WASL results spring to spring, oral fluency results fall, winter, spring, and reading assessment results fall to spring
Review current services to highly capable students and involve parents and teachers in developing an updated model.	By March	Program recommendation report
Serve as coordinator of the Mountain Way Learning Improvement Team, the Elementary Mathematics Committee, and the K–5 Challenge Program.	October–June	Meeting and committee minutes
Lead a teacher book study: *How to Survive and Thrive in the First Three Weeks of School* by Elaine McEwan (2006).	November–March	Participation log
Facilitate an administrative team book study of *Research on Educational Innovations* (4th Edition) by Arthur K. Ellis (2005).	November–March	Participation log

(Continued)

(Continued)

	Time Line	Completion Indicators
Staff Supervision and Evaluation		
Complete teacher observations and professional growth plan meetings as required.	October–May	Observation reports and teacher professional growth plans
Hold goal review meetings, which include an analysis of WASL assessment results, with certificated staff members fall, winter, and spring.	September–June	Goal meeting dates and notes
Visit K–5 classrooms and the PE, library, and music programs regularly.	September–June	Visitation log
School Management and Finance		
Facilitate the development of a K–12 student-parent handbook.	By the end of the next school year	Completed handbook
Upgrade school security measures as required by state regulations.	September–June	Emergency drill log, emergency protocols, emergency handbook
Work with a staff team to develop a new student dismissal system to increase efficiency, integrate with revised bus schedules, and improve student behavior and safety.	January	New system in place and functioning smoothly
Manage the building budget, state inservice grant, highly capable allocation, and related funds competently.	July–June	Budget reports show expenditures within allocations

116

	Time Line	Completion Indicators
Student and Parent Services		
Participate in student study and child study team meetings.	September–June	Meeting reports
Serve as an advisor to the school-parent group People Interested in Kids (PIK).	September–June	Meeting agendas
Spend time with students by sponsoring a fifth-grade Game and Art Club, a weekly Grades 4 and 5 Lunch Bunch, and weekly Primary Talented Tiger Meetings.	September–June	Weekly calendar and bulletin board photos
Provide information to parents through dissemination of school handbook, monthly calendars, bulletins, and bimonthly newsletters.	September–June	Copies of calendars, bulletins, newsletters, and the handbook
Professional Development		
Serve on the editorial advisory board for *Washington State Kappan*, a journal affiliated with Phi Delta Kappa International.	Ongoing	Record of conference calls and meetings
Represent the school district at education service district curriculum director meetings.	November–June	Meeting agendas and minutes
Stay current by attending pertinent workshops and conferences, completing on-line courses, and reading professional books, magazines, journals, and Web sites.	Ongoing	Record of inservice, coursework, readings, and professional readings
Distribute a principal performance rating form to staff.	May	Analysis of survey results

References

Aguayo, R. (1990). *Dr. Deming: The American who taught the Japanese about quality.* New York: Fireside.

Avolio, B. J., Kahai, S., & Dodge, G. (2000). E-leadership and its implications for theory, research and practice. *Leadership Quarterly, 11,* 615–670.

Barth, R. S. (2003). *Lessons learned: Shaping relationships and the culture of the workplace.* Thousand Oaks, CA: Corwin Press.

Beatty, C. A., & Barker Scott, B. A. (2004). *Building smart teams: A roadmap to high performance.* Thousand Oaks, CA: Sage.

Bernhardt, V. L. (2004). *Data analysis for continuous school improvement.* Larchmont, NY: Eye on Education.

Bierema, L. L. (1999, February). The process of the learning organization: Making sense of change. National Association of Secondary School Principals, *NASSP Bulletin, 83,* 46–56.

Blase, J., & Blase, J. (1998). *Handbook of instructional leadership.* Thousand Oaks, CA: Corwin Press.

Blase, J., & Blase, J. (2000). Effective instructional leadership: Teachers' perspectives on how principals promote teaching and learning in schools. *Journal of Educational Administration, 38,* 130–141.

Brubaker, D. L., & Coble, L. D. (2005). *The hidden leader: Leadership lessons on the potential within.* Thousand Oaks, CA: Corwin Press.

Cameron, K. S., Dutton, J. E., & Quinn, R. E. (Eds.). (2003). *Positive organizational scholarship: Foundations of a new discipline.* San Francisco: Berrett-Koehler.

Collins, J. (2001). *Good to great: Why some companies make the leap—and others don't.* New York: Harper Collins.

Collins, J. (2005). *Good to great and the private sectors: A monograph to accompany "Good to great."* New York: Harper Collins.

Council of Chief State School Officers (CCSSO). (1996). *Interstate school leaders licensure consortium: Standards for school leaders.* Washington, DC: Author.

Derrington, M. L. (2007, April). Superintendents effectiveness in evaluation of principals: Arc ISLLC standards the new performance criteria? Paper presented at the meeting of the American Educational Research Association, Chicago, IL.

Derrington, M. L., & Cummings, D. (2008, Winter). Principals and CEO's discover mutual challenges. *The Principal News, 38*(2), 14–15.

Dolan, W. P. (1994). *Restructuring our schools: A primer on systematic change.* Kansas City, MO: Systems & Organizations.

DuFour, R., DuFour, R., Eaker, R., & Karhanek, G. (2004). *Whatever it takes: How professional learning communities respond when kids don't learn.* Bloomington, IN: Solution Tree.

DuFour, R., DuFour, R., Eaker, R., & Many, T. (2006) *Learn by doing.* Bloomington, IN: Solution Tree.

DuFour, R., Eaker, R. (1998). *Professional learning communities at work.* Alexandria, VA: Association for Supervision and Curriculum Development.

Eller, J. (2004). *Effective Group Facilitation in Education.* Thousand Oaks, CA: Corwin Press.

Ellis, A. K. (2005). *Research on educational innovations.* Larchmont, NY: Eye on Education.

Fredrickson, B. L., & Losada, M. F. (2005). Positive affect and the complex dynamics of human flourishing. *American Psychologist, 60,* 678–686.

Fromme, C. A. (2005). An examination of various types of trust through an interdisciplinary trust typology and the implications of these trust types for educators and school system leaders. Unpublished doctoral dissertation, University of Washington, Seattle.

Fullan, M. (1999). *Change forces: The sequel.* Philadelphia: Falmer Press.

Fullan, M. (2001). *The New Meaning of Educational Change.* New York: Teachers College Press.

Fullan, M. (2003). *The moral imperative of school leadership.* Thousand Oaks, CA: Corwin Press.

Fullan, M. (2005). *Leadership and sustainability: Systems thinkers in action.* Thousand Oaks, CA: Corwin Press.

Garvin, D. A. (2000). *Learning in action: A guide to putting the learning organization to work.* Boston: Harvard Business School.

Glaser, J. (2005). *Leading through collaboration: Guiding groups to productive solutions.* Thousand Oaks, CA: Corwin Press.

Glickman, C. D. (1993). *Renewing America's schools: A guide for school based action.* San Francisco: Jossey-Bass.

Goleman, D. (1997). *Emotional intelligence.* New York: Bantam Books.

Goleman, D., Boyatzis, R., & McKee, A. (2002). *Primal leadership: Realizing the power of emotional intelligence.* Boston: Harvard Business School.

Granite Falls School District #322. (2005). Program administrator evaluation instrument. Unpublished document.

Harwayne, S. (1999). *Going public: Priorities and practice at the Manhattan New School.* Portsmouth, NH: Heinemann.

Holcomb, E. (1999). *Getting Excited about Data.* Thousand Oaks, CA: Corwin Press.

Hoyle, J. R., Björk, L. G., Collier, V., & Glass, T. (2005). *The superintendent as CEO: Standards-based performance.* Thousand Oaks, CA: Corwin Press.

Huang, A. H. (2002). E-mail communication and supervisor-subordinate exchange quality: An empirical study. *Human Systems Management, 21,* 193–204.

International Olympic Committee. (2002). Olympic medal slogan: Light the fire within. Retrieve July 17, 2008, from http://www.olympic.org/common/search/

Kayser, T. A. (1990). *Mining for group gold.* El Segundo, CA: Serif Publishing.

Keen, T. R. (2003). *Creating effective and successful teams.* West Lafayette, IN: Ichor Business Books.

LaFasto, F., & Larson, C. E. (2001). *When teams work best: 6,000 team members and leaders tell what it takes to succeed.* Thousand Oaks, CA: Sage.

Lapierre, L. M. (2007). Supervisor trustworthiness and subordinates' willingness to provide extra-role efforts. *Journal of Applied Social Psychology,* 37, 272–297.

Leithwood, K., Aitken, R., & Jantzi, D. (2006). *Making Schools Smarter.* Thousand Oaks, CA: Corwin Press.

Lindle, J. C. (2005). *Twenty strategies for collaborative school leaders.* Larchmont, NY: Eye on Education.

Lindstrom, P., & Speck, M. (2004). *The principal as professional development leader.* Thousand Oaks, CA: Corwin Press.

Loughridge, M., & Tarantino, L. (2005). *Leading effective secondary school reform.* Thousand Oaks, CA: Corwin Press.

Macpherson, R., & Finch, K. (2006, March). The top five qualities you need to advance your career. *The Quill,* 94, 26–27.

Markova, D., & Holland, B. M. (2005, February). Appreciative Inquiry. *The School Administrator,* 62(2), 30–35.

Marzano, R. J., Waters, T., & McNulty, B. A. (2005). *School leadership that works: From research to results.* Aurora, CO: Mid-continent Research for Education and Learning.

McEwan, E. K. (2003). *10 traits of highly effective principals: From good to great performance.* Thousand Oaks, CA: Corwin Press.

McEwan, E. K. (2005). *How to deal with teachers who are angry, troubled, exhausted, or just plain confused.* Thousand Oaks, CA: Corwin Press.

McEwan, E. K. (2006). *How to survive and thrive in the first three weeks of school.* Thousand Oaks, CA: Corwin Press.

McEwan, E. K. (2008). *10 traits of highly effective schools.* Thousand Oaks, CA: Corwin Press.

Michelli, J. (2007). *The Starbucks experience: 5 principles for turning ordinary into extraordinary.* New York: McGraw-Hill.

Nadler, D. A., & Spencer, J. L. (1998). *Executive teams.* San Francisco: Jossey-Bass.

National Association of Elementary School Principals (NAESP). (2001). *Leading Learning Communities: Standards for what principals should know and be able to do.* Alexandria, VA: Author.

Northouse, P. G. (2007). *Leadership: Theory and practice* (4th ed.). Thousand Oaks, CA: Sage.

Peter, L. J. (1977). *Peter's quotations: Ideas for our time.* New York: William Morrow and Company.

Pfeffer, J., & Sutton, R. (1999). The smart-talk trap. *Harvard Business Review* 77(3), 134–142.

Rivero, J. (1998). The role of feedback in executive team effectiveness. In D. A. Nadler & J. L. Spencer (Eds.). *Executive teams* (pp. 180–190). San Francisco: Jossey-Bass.

Salopek, J. (2006). Appreciative Inquiry at 20: Questioning David Cooperrider. *Training and Development, 60,* 21–23. Retrieved December 11, 2006, from ProQuest Research library database.

Scannell, E., & Newstrom, J. (1991). *Still more games trainers play.* New York: McGraw Hill.

Schlechty, P. C. (2006, October). Bureaucracies and learning organizations, *School Administrator, 63,* 62.

Schmoker, M. (2006). *Results NOW.* Alexandria, VA: Association for Supervision and Curriculum Development.

Senge, P. (1993). *The fifth discipline: The art and practice of the learning organization.* London: Century Business.

Sennett, F. (2004). *400 quotable quotes from the world's leading educators.* Thousand Oaks, CA: Corwin Press.

Sergiovani, T. (1987). *The principalship: A reflective practice perspective.* Columbus, OH: Allyn & Bacon.

Shedd, J. B., & Bacharach, S. B. (1991). *Tangled hierarchies: Teachers as professionals and the management of schools.* San Francisco: Jossey-Bass.

Sheppard, B., & Brown, J. (2000, March). So you think team leadership is easy? Training and implementation concerns. *National Association of Secondary School Principals Bulletin, 84,* 71–83.

Smith, M. A., & Canger, J. M. (2004). Effects of supervisor "big five" personality on subordinate attitudes. *Journal of Business and Psychology, 18,* 465–481.

Sparks, D. (2005). *Leading for results: Transforming teaching, learning, and relationships in schools.* Thousand Oaks, CA: Corwin Press. http://www.corwinpress .com/home.nav.

Staub, R. E., II (2001). Leading wholeheartedly. *Journal for Quality and Participation, 24,* 35–37.

Therkelsen, D. J., & Fiebich, C. (2003). The supervisor: The linchpin of employee relations. *Journal of Communication Management, 8,* 120–129.

The New Teacher Project (TNTP). (2006). Improved principal hiring: The Findings and recommendations for urban schools. http://www.tntp.org/files/ TNTP-ImprovedPrincipalHiring-Final.pdf.

Wagner, T. *How Schools Change.* New York: Routledge Falmer.

Walton, E. A. (1998). The importance of trust. In D. A. Nadler & J. L. Spencer (Eds.), *Executive teams* (pp. 135–148). San Francisco: Jossey-Bass.

Washington State Office of Superintendent of Public Instruction. http://www .k12.wa.us/.

Waters, J. T., Marzano, R. J., & McNulty, B. A. (2003). *Balanced leadership: What 30 years of research tells us about the effect of leadership on student achievement.* Aurora, CO: Mid-continent Research for Education and Learning.

Webster's College Dictionary (11th ed.). (2003). New York: Random House.

Wilmore, E. (2002). *Principal leadership: Applying the new Educational Leadership Constituent Council (ELCC) standards.* Thousand Oaks, CA: Corwin Press. http://www.corwinpress.com.

Zemke, R. (1999). Why organizations still aren't learning. *Training,* 36(9), 40–42, 44, 48–49. Retrieved December 13, 2007, from the ProQuest Research Library database.

Suggested Readings

DuFour, R., Eaker, R., & DuFour, R. (Eds.). (2005). *On common ground: The power of professional learning communities.* Bloomington, IN: Solution Tree.

Fitch, L., & Evans, B. (2003). *Tools for teaming: Using quality tools to enhance and improve learning systems.* Yakima, WA: Quality in Education, Inc.

Fredrickson, B. (2001). The role of positive emotions in positive psychology. *American Psychologist, 56,* 218–226.

Gittell, J. A. (2003). A theory of relational coordination. In K. S. Cameron, J. E. Dutton, & R. E. Quinn (Eds.), *Positive organizational scholarship: Foundations of a new discipline* (pp. 279–295). San Francisco: Berrett-Koehler.

Hord, S. M. (2007). Learn in community with others. *Journal of Staff Development, 28*(3).

Luthans, F., & Avolio, B. (2003). Authentic leadership development. In K. Cameron, J. E. Dutton, & Quinn, R. E. (Eds.), *Positive organizational scholarship: Foundations of a new discipline* (pp. 241–258). San Francisco: Berrett-Koehler.

Maxwell, J. C. (2001). *Developing the leader within you workbook.* Nashville, TN: Thomas Nelson.

Mintzberg, H. (1983). *Structures in fives, designing effective organizations.* Englewood Cliffs, NJ: Prentice-Hall Inc.

Nadler, D. A., & Nadler, M. (1998). Performance on the executive team: Managing the unique dynamics and special demands. In D. A. Nadler & J. L. Spencer (Eds.), *Executive teams* (pp. 112–134). San Francisco: Jossey-Bass.

Tool Time for Education. (2002). Choosing and implementing quality improvement tools. Langford International, Molt, MT.

Yandle, B. (1992). Does anyone still care? *SuperVision, 53,* 14–16.

Index

CORWIN PRESS